THE LEADERSHIP PROGRESS

How to Smoothly Transition from
Supervisor to Team Leader to Manager

A Comprehensive Guide to Developing
Essential Leadership

TR. RALPH

DEDICATION
To My Son

TABLE OF CONTENTS

Introduction...5

Part I: Transition
Understanding the ROLES...10
The Process of Transition...18
Career Development...22
New Leaders Challenges...24

Part II: Foundational Skills
The Crucial Mindset of Achieving...26
Planning and Organization...30
Decision Making...33
Motivation...36
Develop Your Team...42
Show Adaptability Managing Stress...49

Part III: Enhancing Communication and Relationships
Communication Skills...55
Building and Maintaining Relationships...62
Encouraging Teamwork...70
Trust...78

Part IV: Advanced Leadership Skills
Support and Influence...84
Working for the Results...89
Execution...96
Safety Talk...104

Part V: The Impact of Decisions, Behavior, and Continuous Improvement
The Impact of Decisions...109
Behavior, Dress code, and Representation...121
Navigating Change and Improvement...133

"The Leadership Progress" is more than just a book; it is a comprehensive roadmap for those aspiring to excel in their leadership roles. Whether you are stepping into a supervisory position or advancing to higher levels of management, this book provides the tools, knowledge, and confidence to lead with excellence and integrity. This guide takes you step by step through every aspect of your leadership journey, covering the smallest details to ensure you are fully equipped for success. It delves into the nuances of leadership transitions, helping you understand the distinct roles and responsibilities at each stage. By offering practical strategies and insights, it addresses the common challenges new leaders face, ensuring you are prepared to navigate these obstacles effectively.

INTRODUCTION

The difficulties that leaders face as they rise through the rank's changes from one level to the next. Did you know that nearly half of all newly promoted leaders struggle to adjust to their new roles? While there are universal skills that work across different levels of authority, there are also cases where the talents needed for success at one level can hinder a leader's performance at the next. Take for example supervisors who has managed successfully with a smooth style of extra friendliness. Easy-going supervisors often have friendly and approachable demeanors, which can build good relationships with their team members. However, as a manager, there is a need to balance this friendliness with authority and decisiveness. It can be challenging for someone used to being liked by their team to assert authority and make tough decisions that may not always be popular.

The primary challenges encountered by leaders at every level are highlighted in this book, as are the necessary abilities for success.

<u>The following is a list of the most pressing issues facing today's leaders who want to progress.</u>

Skill Set Variation: Each role requires a different set of skills and competencies. While a supervisor may focus more on overseeing day-to-day tasks and ensuring they are completed efficiently, a superintendent (team Leader) might be more concerned with larger-scale operations and coordination, and a manager may need to handle strategic planning, team development, and resource allocation. Moving between these roles often necessitates acquiring new skills and adapting to different responsibilities.

Hierarchical Differences: The levels of authority and scope of responsibility vary between these roles. Supervisors typically report to superintendents (team leaders), who in turn might report to managers or higher-level executives. Moving upward often means dealing with broader organizational concerns, navigating more complex decision-making processes, and managing larger teams or departments, that's why adjusting to these hierarchical shifts can be challenging.

Interpersonal Dynamics: Each role involves different relationships with subordinates, peers, and higher-ups. Supervisors often have more direct interactions with frontline employees, while superintendents and managers may need to focus on building relationships with other managers, executives, and stakeholders. Transitioning between these roles requires adapting to new interpersonal dynamics and communication styles.

Expectation and Accountability: With each step up the hierarchy, the expectations and levels of accountability increase. Superintendents and managers are typically held responsible for not only their own performance but also the performance of their teams or departments. Transitioning between these roles involves understanding and meeting higher levels of expectation and being accountable for broader outcomes.

Organizational Culture: Different levels within an organization often have distinct cultures and norms. Moving between roles may require adjusting to new cultural expectations, new vocabulary, and more insight on "what is really going on". Adapting to new ways of decision-making processes, and ways of working can take time and effort.

Learning Curve: Transitioning between roles involves a learning curve. In other words, a time needed at which someone gains proficiency in a new position, as individuals need to familiarize themselves with new responsibilities, processes, and expectations. This learning process can be challenging and may require support and guidance from mentors, colleagues, or training programs.

Your development is your responsibility: Self-improvement is becoming more and more important in today's quickly changing environment. For many companies, the emergence of the new generation has accelerated this change since young workers are eager to accept more responsibility and more influence over their career path and growth. Your career is ultimately in your hands, and only you are responsible for it. You are the only one who can identify your interests and goals. You are the only one who can take advantage of the chances your boss has identified for you. <u>It is your responsibility.</u>

Self-improvement: To make significant progress in any field, one must put in the time and effort required over an extended period. Not only does development need personal dedication and ingenuity, but also the input and encouragement of others.

When you go through the process of developing your competencies, you can:
   a) Clearly define your growth target so that you may direct your efforts toward a reasonable goal.
   b) Develop a clear picture of your present level of performance to appropriately highlight where your time and attention should be spent.
   c) Create a detailed plan with specific actions.
   d) Highlight possible roadblocks, key milestones, and time frames.
   e) Create a support system of people and resources to help you along the journey.
   f) Develop a method to keep yourself motivated and on track.

Prioritize Your Current Position First: To begin, think about where you are now. Prioritize any gaps between your present performance and the needs of your position when taking development actions. Consider all facets of your job. Is everything you do flawless, or are there areas in which you might improve? Compared to your peers, how well are you doing?

Have you received comments in your performance evaluations from bosses or colleagues or others indicating any areas for improvement?

Taking the time to honestly evaluate the root cause of your difficulty will assist you in developing a focused and inspiring target more quickly and efficiently.

Prioritize Your Future Plans Second: When you're interested in a position elsewhere in the company, search for information in the job postings that will help you figure out what qualities are most important. To help you figure out and evaluate your development efforts, it's good to get help from other people. You might look for people who are currently doing what you want to do, or who display the talents you want to develop. Invite them to talk about their long-term aspirations. Learn how they developed and refined their skills, including training or mentors.

Know What You Have: Once you've identified your growth goal, then you will become aware of your actual competence level. This will help you identify how you will bridge the performance gap between your current skills and goal in the future. There are two basic methods for increasing awareness. First, you may analyze your own skill set, second, you can get feedback from others, such as superiors, trainers, or mentors.

Ask Your Boss: An important source of information about your present skills and future potential is your boss. As a mentor, he or she will assist discover your blind spots and help you develop or build on your strengths so you may be more productive in your job. During your yearly performance evaluation with your boss, you have the chance to reflect on your strengths and areas for improvement, all while formulating a strategy for moving forward in your career. Overall, transitioning between supervisor, superintendent, and manager roles requires individuals to be adaptable, proactive in acquiring new skills, and willing to navigate the complexities of organizational structures and dynamics. It's not necessarily that it's inherently difficult, but rather that it involves significant adjustments and growth.

In this book you will learn" how to transition" from one level to the next, but more importantly to understand "what is your role as leader and how to succeed".

Part I: Transitions

Transitions are a part of life. They are the bridge between the old and the new, and they often lead to growth and transformation.

Susan Wiggs

UNDERSTANDING THE ROLES

Transitioning through various levels of leadership within an organization involves distinct roles and responsibilities that contribute to the overall success and efficiency of the team. Each leadership level, from supervisors to superintendents to managers, has specific functions that build upon one another, ensuring a seamless operation and continuous growth. This awareness empowers you to not only excel in your current role but also prepare effectively for the challenges and opportunities that lie ahead.

A supervisor for example, transitions from being merely a team member to becoming a team leader, taking on the responsibility of building relationships to achieve tasks effectively. This role involves managing conflicts efficiently and resolving challenges successfully. At the superintendent level, the leader selects and leads a supervisory team, integrates diverse interests and ideas, navigates organizational politics, and devises execution plans through supervisors.

And then at the managerial level, the leader here defines and prioritizes both long-term and short-term objectives and compromises, establishes strategies, maintains open communication with other departments, and continually raises performance standards.

To understand the roles more, lets dive right into it:

SUPERVISOR

Becomes a Team Leader Instead of Just a Team Member

A **supervisor**'s transition from being merely a team member to a team leader marks a significant evolution in their professional journey. This role expansion is pivotal as it involves not only a change in responsibilities but also a fundamental shift in workplace dynamics and personal accountability. Unlike team members who primarily focus on executing tasks, a supervisor must step up to take charge of the entire project's trajectory. This includes planning, delegating tasks, and making pivotal decisions that will affect the project outcome and team morale. And in a unionized setting, supervisors take on an additional responsibility: ensuring the fair application of established procedures and collective bargaining agreements. This commitment fosters a positive work environment and promotes trust between employees and management with an added weight on the supervisor's shoulder.

Perhaps the most influential role a supervisor as a team leader can play is that of a role model. Furthermore, the supervisor's own work ethic, attitude, and professionalism set the standard for the rest of the team. And commitment to these qualities can inspire similar behavior among team members, nurturing a culture of excellence and integrity.

Constructs Relationships to Accomplish Tasks

Building strong relationships is central to a supervisor's effectiveness. These relationships can be with team members, peers, higher management, or even external stakeholders.

A **supervisor** who can navigate these relationships skillfully can enhance team performance and facilitate smoother project execution. In the same way, regular and open communication helps to build trust and clarifies expectations. This can involve structured meetings as well as more informal conversations. Likewise, open communication also includes encouraging feedback from others, which can lead to improvements and innovations. Effective supervisors also cultivate a sense of unity and purpose among team members. This can involve team-building exercises, shared goals, and collective rewards. Overall, a cohesive team is more likely to overcome obstacles and maintain high productivity levels.

Although, while building close relationships is important, maintaining professional boundaries is equally critical. This ensures that decisions are based on objective criteria rather than personal biases, which helps in upholding the integrity of the supervisory role.

Manages Conflict Effectively

Supervisors inevitably face conflict within their teams. Because collaboration can breed disagreement, mastering conflict resolution skills is paramount. Effective conflict resolution involves a balanced approach that addresses the issue while maintaining team harmony and morale. Generally speaking, early identification of potential conflicts—whether they stem from resource allocation, personal differences, or task-related issues—can prevent them from escalating. This requires a keen awareness of team dynamics and individual behaviors.

Resolves Challenges with Success

A **supervisor**'s ability to effectively tackle challenges is a testament to their leadership and problem-solving skills. Successful resolution of challenges not only drives the team's progress but also builds credibility and trust among team members. Before addressing a challenge, a supervisor must thoroughly understand it, and this involves gathering information, consulting with experts if necessary, and assessing the resources available.

In conclusion, a supervisor's role is multifaceted and demands a dynamic approach to leadership. The supervisor level is the initiation of your future roles. Your success as a supervisor is a great indication of what is coming.

SUPERINTENDENT (TEAM LEADER)

Selects and Leads a Supervisory Team

A **superintendent**'s foundational responsibility is to assemble and direct a supervisory team capable of implementing the organization's goals effectively. This involves identifying potential leaders who not only possess the necessary technical skills but also embody the leadership qualities that align with the organization's values and culture. And this process of selection is a meticulous one that evaluates candidates on their past performance, leadership potential, and their ability to work collaboratively. However, once the team is in place, the superintendent takes on the role of a mentor and guide, creating an environment where supervisors are empowered to make decisions and encouraged to develop their leadership styles within the framework of the organization's objectives.

Incorporates Different Interests and Ideas

A key role of the **superintendent** is to synthesize diverse interests and ideas into a coherent strategic vision. This requires a deep understanding of the various stakeholders involved—including employees, management, and external partners—and the ability to navigate differing opinions and priorities. By facilitating open dialogue and encouraging inclusive decision-making processes, the superintendent ensures that all voices are heard and valued. This collaborative approach not only enriches the planning and implementation phases but also builds a stronger, more committed team. The resultant strategy benefits from the collective insights and expertise of the entire group, leading to more innovative and effective outcomes.

Manages Supervisory Politics

The realm of supervisory politics involves navigating the complex interpersonal and interdepartmental dynamics that can influence decision-making and organizational effectiveness. A superintendent must adeptly manage these dynamics to maintain harmony and drive the organization's agenda.

This includes mediating conflicts, balancing power structures, and ensuring transparency in communications. By cultivating a political climate that values integrity and fairness, the **superintendent** helps prevent the personal agendas and power struggles that can undermine collective goals. Undoubtedly, effective management of supervisory politics reinforces a culture of trust and cooperation that is essential for any successful organization.

Outlines Execution Plans Through Supervisors

Clear execution plans will bridge the gap between strategic goals and actionable steps. Superintendents play a critical role in this process. They act as the linchpin, ensuring high-level objectives are translated into practical, day-to-day operations. By crafting well-defined execution plans, they empower teams to understand and efficiently implement strategic goals across all organizational levels. This allows everyone to contribute meaningfully toward achieving the organization's overall vision.

The **superintendent** develops detailed action plans that delineate responsibilities, timelines, and resources, which are communicated to supervisors for execution. This structured approach helps maintain clarity and focus at every level of the organization, facilitating effective monitoring and coordination of tasks. As a result, supervisors equipped with clear guidelines and objectives, are better prepared to manage their teams and achieve desired outcomes. Moreover, by regularly reviewing these plans with supervisors, the superintendent can assess progress, make necessary adjustments, and provide support where needed to keep the organization on track toward its goals.

MANAGER

Defines and Prioritizes Long- and Short-Term Objectives and Compromises

A critical role of a **manager** is to define clear objectives that align with the organization's overall mission and break these down into achievable short-term and long-term goals. This strategic prioritization ensures that resources are allocated efficiently and that the team remains focused on the most impactful tasks. Additionally, the ability to compromise where necessary—balancing ideal outcomes with practical constraints—allows a manager to navigate challenges flexibly and maintain progress. This balancing act requires a deep understanding of the organization's priorities and an ability to negotiate and adjust plans as scenarios evolve, thereby ensuring sustained advancement towards goals despite inevitable obstacles.

Establishes Strategy

Establishing strategy involves not only setting goals but also deciding the best path to achieve these objectives. A **manager** must consider various strategic alternatives and select the approach that optimally aligns with the organization's strengths and the external environment. This process includes thorough market analysis, risk assessment, and resource evaluation to formulate a comprehensive action plan that guides the entire team. By clearly articulating this strategy and the rationale behind it, the manager ensures that all team members are unified and motivated, understanding their roles in the larger context of the organization's ambitions.

Openness and Communications with Other Departments

Effective managers understand that openness and proactive communication with other departments are key to organizational success.

By promoting a culture of transparency, **managers** help ensure that information flows freely across departmental boundaries, enhancing collaboration and innovation. Regular interactions and updates between departments can prevent silos and ensure that different parts of the organization work cohesively towards common objectives. Eventually, this openness not only improves efficiency but also contributes to a more adaptable and agile organizational structure, where responses to external changes are swift and informed by a holistic understanding of organizational challenges and capabilities.

Raises the Bar

Effective leadership hinges on the ability to establish and continually elevate performance standards. Managers play a critical role in this process. Through the strategic setting of objectives and the ongoing encouragement of professional development, they present a work environment where exceeding expectations becomes a driving force. This focus on continuous improvement empowers teams to achieve their full potential and contribute meaningfully to the organization's overall success. This involves setting ambitious yet achievable goals, providing the necessary resources for success, and fostering an environment that rewards innovation and excellence. Moreover, encouraging continual professional development and learning also helps maintain a high-performance culture that adapt resilient to market changes and technological advancements. In doing so, **managers** ensure their teams are not complacent but are driven to continuously improve and excel.

Maintains a Global Vision

In today's interconnected world, maintaining a global vision is essential for **managers**. This means thinking beyond local or immediate considerations to understand how global trends and dynamics could impact the organization. A manager with a global vision takes into account international markets, cultural differences, and global economic factors when executing strategies.

This broad perspective helps in identifying new opportunities and threats from beyond traditional boundaries and in crafting strategies that are robust across different geographic and market conditions. Such a worldview is crucial for ensuring that the organization not only survives but thrives in the competitive global marketplace.

THE PROCESS OF TRANSITION

Show your intent for moving upward!

One often-missed secret weapon for career advancement within any organization is proactively expressing your ambitions. It's a simple yet powerful concept: <u>if you don't voice your desire for growth, your potential for promotion might go unnoticed</u>. By clearly communicating your career aspirations, you take control of your professional journey and position yourself for future opportunities. Don't be afraid to advocate for yourself – it demonstrates initiative and commitment to the company's success. Furthermore, by proactively communicating your desire to advance, you make it clear that you are both capable and eager to take on new challenges, ensuring that you are considered when opportunities for promotion arise. On the other hand, you must show them through actions, not just words, that you are worthy of the opportunity, and to be considered, you need to consistently demonstrate your value and few other qualities:

First, **demonstrate consistent excellence in your current role**. This involves not only meeting but exceeding expectations and consistently delivering high-quality results. And then show your ability to handle responsibilities efficiently and be a reliable asset to your team.

Next, **seek opportunities for professional development**. This could involve taking on additional responsibilities, attending relevant workshops or training sessions, and staying updated with industry trends. Enhancing your skill set and knowledge base makes you a more valuable candidate for higher positions.

Ex: John, an IT support specialist, enrolled in advanced cybersecurity courses to enhance his skills. He also attended industry conferences and workshops to stay updated on the latest trends. By earning relevant certifications and demonstrating his new knowledge through improved security protocols at his company, John made himself an obvious choice for the senior IT analyst role when it became available.

Building a strong professional network within the company. Establish relationships with colleagues, mentors, and leaders across different departments. Networking can provide valuable insights into the company's inner workings and make you more visible to decision-makers.

Ex: Sarah, an account executive, made a point to attend company events and join cross-departmental projects. She developed strong relationships with colleagues from different teams and sought mentorship from senior leaders. When a team leader position opened up, her well-established network and reputation for collaboration helped her secure the role.

Additionally, and even more important than anything else, **communicate your career aspirations with your manager**. Your current boss is your best ambassador for your endorsement, and he is your best promoter. Rather than bringing up your career goals in a casual hallway conversation, schedule a dedicated meeting with your manager or during performance reviews or a one-on-one meeting. Express your interest in advancing within the company. Seek feedback on areas for improvement and create a development plan to address these areas. Furthermore, come to the meeting with a clear understanding of your achievements, strengths, and areas for growth. Be specific about your career aspirations and articulate how these align with the company's objectives. Explain why you are passionate about your desired path and how you envision your progression benefiting the organization.

Seek constructive feedback and guidance from your manager on what skills or experiences you need to develop further. Similarly, express your willingness to take on new challenges or responsibilities that can help you gain the necessary experience. And then, propose the creation of a development plan that outlines your short-term and long-term goals, including actionable steps and timelines. In the same way, demonstrate your commitment to your professional growth by regularly following up with your manager to discuss your progress and any additional support you may need. This ongoing communication shows your dedication and helps keep your career development on track.

Moreover, **take initiative to solve problems and propose innovative ideas**. Show that you can think strategically and contribute to the company's growth. Taking the lead on projects or suggesting improvements demonstrates your readiness for more significant responsibilities.

Ex: Emily, a product designer, noticed inefficiencies in the product development process. She took the initiative to research and propose a new project management tool that streamlined communication and task assignments. By successfully leading the implementation of this tool and demonstrating its benefits, Emily showcased her strategic thinking and leadership potential, leading to her promotion to product design lead.

Finally, **be patient and persistent**. Career advancement may take time, there might be people ahead of you in the queue, however, by consistently working towards your goals, staying proactive, and maintaining a positive attitude, you will eventually see your efforts pay off.

Ex: David, a customer service representative, consistently sought ways to improve his skills and contribute to his team. Despite facing several setbacks and knowing that there are people ahead of him with more date, he remained dedicated to his professional development. Over time, his persistence paid off, and he was eventually promoted to customer service manager. David's journey highlighted the importance of resilience and long-term commitment to career growth.

Beyond the obvious reasons of achieving a higher position at all levels, here are a few additional motivations of **why you should progress in ranks.**

Expanding your scope of responsibility and impact

As you transition from one level of team leadership to another, the scope of your responsibilities broadens and your impact on the organization becomes more significant. This evolution is not merely an increase in the number of tasks you oversee but a profound transformation in the nature of your role and the influence you wield within the company. It is more than just taking on additional projects or managing larger teams. It encompasses a strategic deepening of your involvement in the company's core operations and a shift towards more complex decision-making processes. As you climb higher up the leadership ladder, your focus shifts from handling day-to-day tasks to making long-term strategic decisions that will shape the direction of the organization. In this new higher role, you are required to integrate various streams of information from across the company to guide these decisions. This means not only keeping up with the immediate needs of your own team but also understanding how they fit into the broader objectives of the organization. Your decisions will now potentially impact multiple departments and stakeholders, requiring a holistic approach to management.

Enhancing Your Impact within the Organization

With greater responsibility comes the opportunity to create a larger impact. This enhanced impact can be seen in several ways, first, as a more advanced leader, you have a seat at the table where the most crucial business decisions are made. Your insights and opinions can significantly influence the organization's strategies and policies. You have the power to set standards for behavior and ethics within the company. The example you set can either reinforce a positive workplace culture or undermine it, thus impacting employee engagement and productivity.

Furthermore, at a higher level, you are also in a better position to drive and champion innovative ideas and push for changes that can lead to significant improvements in how the organization operates. Transitioning from one leadership level to another is an exciting, albeit challenging, journey. It requires a new set of skills and a greater understanding of the complex dynamics within a large organization. Your ability to manage these expanded responsibilities effectively will not only impact your career but also the success of the company as a whole. By embracing these challenges and continuously seeking personal and professional growth, you can ensure that your influence within the organization is both positive and profound.

CAREER DEVELOPMENT

Create a Plan

Embarking on a leadership transition begins with a foundational step: crafting a thorough plan. This plan should clearly define your transition goals, pinpoint the skills and knowledge you need to acquire, and lay out the specific actions you'll take to achieve these objectives. It's important to set both short-term milestones and long-term objectives and consider potential challenges and how you might overcome them. Your plan will act as a roadmap, helping you navigate through the complexities of stepping into a leadership role, ensuring that you cover all necessary aspects systematically.

Seek Support

Transitioning into leadership can be daunting, and seeking support from mentors, peers, or a professional coach can be incredibly beneficial. These individuals can provide you with valuable insights, advice, and encouragement. They can help you understand the nuances of effective leadership within your specific context and offer guidance based on their own experiences. Support networks also serve as a sounding board for your ideas and concerns, providing you with diverse perspectives that can enhance your decision-making skills and confidence.

Measure Progress

As you put your plan into action, it's vital to consistently measure your progress. This means assessing how effectively you're acquiring the necessary skills and reaching your established milestones. Regular assessment helps you stay on track and make necessary adjustments to your strategy. It also allows you to reflect on your learning and growth, which is essential for continuous improvement. Setting up specific criteria for success for each stage of your plan will enable you to see more clearly what works, what doesn't, and how close you are to reaching your leadership goals.

Learn from Work Experience

One of the best ways to prepare for a leadership role is to learn actively from your current work experiences. Take on projects that challenge you and allow you to build new skills. Seek opportunities that expose you to leadership tasks, such as managing a team, coordinating a project, or representing your department at company meetings. Hands-on experience is invaluable as it not only enhances your skills but also helps you understand the practical challenges of leading a team.

Learning from Others

Observing and learning from the experiences of other leaders is another effective way to prepare for your transition. This can include studying the leadership styles of your superiors or other respected leaders within or outside your organization. Pay attention to how they handle decision-making, conflict resolution, team motivation, and other key aspects of leadership. You can also learn from the mistakes and successes of these leaders through case studies, biographies, and real-life stories to gain insights into what might work or not in your own leadership approach.

Education

Formal education and training can also play a pivotal role in preparing for a leadership transition. This might involve taking courses on management and leadership, attending workshops, or participating in relevant conferences and seminars. These educational opportunities provide you with theoretical knowledge and practical skills in leadership. They also keep you updated with the latest trends and best practices in leadership and management that you can apply in your new role. By creating a detailed plan, seeking out support, measuring your progress, gaining hands-on experience, learning from others, and pursuing formal education, you can develop the necessary skills and confidence to successfully step into a leadership role and thrive.

NEW LEADERS' CHALLENGES

Handling Increased Pressure, Delegating Effectively, and Managing Upwards.

When transitioning to a higher level of responsibility in a leading role, professionals face a unique set of challenges that test their resolve, adaptability, and skill. Understanding these challenges and preparing for them can significantly improve one's effectiveness and ease the transition.

The first step in a successful transition is recognizing that challenges are an inevitable part of moving into a more senior position. These challenges often stem from increased expectations and responsibilities that require new skills and a greater breadth of knowledge.

Management challenges could range from handling a larger team to dealing with complex projects that have a broader impact on the company's success. In short, it's vital to approach these challenges with a proactive mindset, seeking to identify potential problems early and develop strategies to address them.

Increased Pressure

With greater responsibility comes increased pressure to perform. This pressure can manifest in several ways, including tighter deadlines, higher stakes decisions, and greater scrutiny from upper management and stakeholders. To cope with this increased pressure, you must maintain a clear focus on your objectives and priorities.

Effective stress management strategies, such as structured problem-solving, regular communication with your team and peers, and time management can help mitigate the impact of this pressure. Additionally, maintaining a work-life balance is essential to sustain your performance over the long term without burning out.

Knowing How to Delegate Effectively

Among the most crucial competencies for successful management is the art of delegation. Mastering this skill not only streamlines your workload but also empowers your team members for a smooth transition as you take on higher responsibilities. Effective delegation goes beyond simply assigning tasks. It involves equipping your team with the necessary resources and authority to excel in their assigned duties. This will create a sense of ownership and accountability, leading to a more productive and empowered workforce. You need to match tasks with the team member's skills and capabilities and ensure there is clear communication about expectations and outcomes. This not only helps in managing the increased workload but also aids in developing your team's capabilities and confidence, which is crucial for the overall growth of the organization.

Managing Upwards

Managing upwards is another vital skill for anyone in a transitioning management role. This involves managing your relationship with your own superiors in a way that encourages mutual respect and understanding. Effective upward management includes regularly updating superiors on progress, being transparent about challenges, and seeking their advice when necessary. It also involves advocating for your team's needs and ensuring that upper management understands and supports your strategic vision and the operational requirements needed to achieve it.

By following these practices, you can build trust and collaboration with your superiors, ultimately propelling your team and yourself towards achieving your goals.

Part II: Foundational Skills

Whether you think you can, or you think you can't — you're right.

Henry Ford

THE CRUTIAL MINDSET OF ACHIEVING

Have you ever felt discouraged by a setback, thinking "I'm just not good at this"? Or perhaps you've witnessed someone embrace a challenge with the attitude, "This is tough, but I can learn it!" These contrasting perspectives highlight the power of mindsets, a concept pioneered by renowned psychologist Carol Dweck. Born in 1947, Dr. Dweck's extensive research on motivation delves into how our underlying beliefs about intelligence and learning can dramatically impact our success. Let's explore the two mindsets she identifies and how they can influence your personal and professional growth.

A "fixed mindset" or a "growth mindset"

According to Dweck, those with a **fixed mindset** believe that their intelligence, abilities, and talents are static traits that cannot be significantly changed. They often view challenges and obstacles as threats, avoiding them to prevent failure or the appearance of incompetence. People with this mindset see effort as unnecessary or even counterproductive, believing that without natural abilities, there is nothing else you can do. They also tend to take criticism personally and feel threatened by the success of others, which can lead to feelings of envy and insecurity. Ultimately, a fixed mindset can severely limit personal growth and potential by discouraging learning, resilience, and the willingness to tackle new challenges.

In contrast, individuals with a **growth mindset** believe that their intelligence, abilities, and talents can be developed through dedication, effort, and learning. They embrace challenges, viewing them as opportunities to expand their capabilities and knowledge. Those with a growth mindset persist in the face of setbacks, recognizing effort as an essential part of their development. They regard criticism as constructive feedback that can lead to improvement and find inspiration in the success of others, using it as a learning opportunity. By adopting a growth mindset, people open themselves to endless possibilities for personal and professional advancement, continually evolving and enhancing their skills and understanding. This mindset prepares you to a resilient and proactive approach to life and learning, making it a powerful tool for achieving lasting success and fulfillment.

Carol Dweck's groundbreaking research on the growth mindset presents a transformative approach that can significantly influence an individual's potential for personal and professional growth. The growth mindset, characterized by the belief that abilities and intelligence can be developed, is especially crucial for leadership roles within a company. A team leader can adopt and nurture a growth mindset by integrating several key practices into their leadership style and overall professional development strategy.

So, how can we embrace the "growth mindset"?

Embrace Challenges: Team leaders should view new projects, roles, and challenges not as threats, but as invaluable opportunities to learn and expand their skill set. Approaching each new endeavor with curiosity and a willingness to explore new strategies can dramatically enhance personal growth and team performance.

Persist Through Obstacles: Encountering setbacks is an unavoidable aspect of every professional journey, especially in leadership roles. Recognizing that obstacles can serve as steppingstones in your learning process is crucial. When you take the time to analyze failures, understanding what went wrong and how to improve, you not only build resilience but also enhance your capabilities. This process serves as a powerful example for your team, demonstrating that growth often arises from overcoming challenges.

Value Effort: In a growth-oriented environment, the focus shifts from solely celebrating successes to recognizing the value of persistent effort and commitment to continuous improvement. By celebrating these efforts, a culture is cultivated where perseverance is seen as a direct path to mastery, encouraging the team to remain dedicated and motivated, even in the face of challenges.

Seek and Provide Constructive Feedback: Constructive feedback is a cornerstone of the growth mindset. Actively seeking feedback on one's own performance and providing thoughtful, developmental feedback to others promotes an environment of continuous improvement and open communication.

Learn from the Success of Others: Instead of viewing colleagues' successes as a threat, seeing them as a source of inspiration and learning is vital. Analyzing what contributed to their success can provide valuable insights that can be adapted to one's own strategy for growth.

Cultivate a Team Culture of Learning: creating ongoing learning and development is essential. By facilitating knowledge sharing and providing resources and opportunities for professional growth, a leader sustains an environment that values curiosity and proactive learning.

Invest in Personal Development: Leaders must also commit to their own continuous learning by engaging in professional development activities, staying abreast of industry trends, and enhancing their leadership skills. This personal growth not only enhances their capabilities but also sets a strong example for their team.

Adapt and Innovate: Encouraging creative thinking and innovation within the team helps in exploring new possibilities and improving solutions. This practice supports the company's adaptability and resilience in a changing business landscape.

Mentorship and Networking: Engaging with mentors who embody the growth mindset can provide invaluable guidance. Offering the same guidance to others not only builds a supportive network within the company but also enriches the mentor's own understanding and expertise.

Reflect on Progress: Regular reflection on both achievements and areas for improvement helps in setting clear goals and identifying new areas for development. This reflection ensures that growth remains a constant pursuit and helps in aligning with the company's objectives.

By adopting these practices, a team leader can effectively leverage a growth mindset to not only advance their own career but also enhance the dynamics and productivity of their team. This holistic approach to leadership and development underscores the importance of continuous learning, adaptability, and striving for excellence—qualities indispensable for successful leadership.

PLANNING AND ORGANIZATION

Planning and Organization are essential blueprints that help you achieve your overarching goals. Good leaders know how to construct these plans and establish mechanisms to ensure everyone collaborates effectively. Without adequate planning, you may find yourself redoing tasks, losing motivation, or failing to meet your targets. Different organizational roles, such as supervisors, superintendents, and managers, each have unique planning responsibilities that contribute to the success of the organization.

Supervisors are pivotal in planning work effectively, establishing action planning layers, and coordinating tasks across functions by sequencing and setting cutoff times. They need a sharp sense for anticipating problems and identifying resources to address them. By initiating methods to assess progress, such as setting deadlines, time limits, and budgets, supervisors ensure project timelines and financial constraints are respected. This proactive approach distinguishes great supervisors, ensuring projects stay on track and within budget, ultimately leading to efficient and effective results.

Superintendents play a crucial role in setting realistic estimates for the resources required, such as staffing and budget and to meet work goals. Their expertise lies in noting and categorizing risks and variables within plans, which significantly aids in preemptive problem-solving. By establishing clear and attainable deadlines, they create strategies that strike a balance between long-term planning and meeting the immediate demands of the company. This dual focus ensures that strategic goals are continuously pursued without neglecting the day-to-day operations essential to the company's stability and growth. With their ability to foresee potential obstacles and proactively address them, superintendents contribute to the seamless integration of strategic vision and operational efficiency.

Managers have the task of translating broad strategies into specific targets and action plans. They create or adjust the current routines of their departments to align with strategic goals. This involves ensuring the integration and alignment of activities across various functions and locations within the department, encompassing staff, budget, and productivity considerations. Managers play a key role in adapting departmental structures to better meet strategic objectives and respond to changing conditions.

Planning and Organization In DEPTH

Effective Work Planning

Planning involves making a schedule and adhering to it, evaluating one's adherence to this plan, and identifying areas for improvement. Recognizing the value of one's time and assigning monetary value to it can help prioritize tasks that offer the greatest return on investment. Managers are encouraged to review their schedules periodically to identify time wasters and optimize productivity by aligning tasks with their most productive times of the day or week.

Establishing Action Planning Layers

Action planning involves creating a detailed task list and sticking to it. Setting objectives for both the entire project and its sub-tasks helps in managing project progression effectively. Involving team members in developing a visual measurement system that is regularly updated ensures that key priorities are always in focus and that the entire team is aligned on project goals.

Coordinating Tasks Across Functions

Effective coordination includes identifying necessary tasks and the resources required for upcoming projects. Developing a master plan helps in tracking multiple simultaneous tasks and managing resource allocation to prevent overextension.

Gathering input from all relevant parties ensures that everyone's needs are incorporated into departmental plans, enhancing overall project coherence and execution.

Anticipating Problems

Proactive management involves anticipating potential issues and planning resources and staffing contingencies to mitigate risks. Regular discussions about medium and long-term objectives with superiors help in aligning project goals with organizational objectives and preparing for factors outside one's control.

Assessing Progress

Initiating methods for progress assessment, such as budget monitoring and setting performance metrics, helps in evaluating the success of a project. Dividing large projects into phases with specific benchmarks allows for ongoing evaluation and necessary adjustments, ensuring projects stay aligned with the company's strategic and financial cycles.

Balancing Planning and Immediate Needs

Strategic planning must also consider immediate operational demands. Regular reviews of resource allocation and identifying major constraints are essential in ensuring that the strategies implemented do not just focus on long-term goals but also address current operational needs. Engaging teams in identifying which activities are essential and which can be scaled back prevents redundancy and ensures that resources are focused where they are most needed.

By understanding and implementing these varied aspects of planning across different organizational roles, leaders can ensure that their teams are not only prepared for immediate challenges but are also strategically aligned for long-term success.

DECISION MAKING

Leaders at all levels increasingly grapple with a relentless influx of new information and face intricate and formidable challenges that demand resolution. The modern landscape of rapid technology advancements and instantaneous communications, coupled with a global perspective on operations, necessitates a blend of swift action and thorough research to make sound decisions. Crafting decisions that minimize risk while maximizing efficiency and effectiveness requires the ability to think clearly and strategically, making well-founded judgments based on relevant facts and inputs from stakeholders.

Supervisors must gather sufficient information to effectively tackle problems, employing logical reasoning in their decision-making. Adhering to organizational guidelines and directives ensures consistency in their actions. By exploring various problem-solving methods, supervisors can address issues creatively and effectively. With a solid foundation of information, logical reasoning, and adherence to guidelines, supervisors can navigate complexities and drive their teams toward successful outcomes.

Superintendents delve into the core causes of issues, making decisions sometimes with limited information or data. They consistently confront and scrutinize problems regardless of the circumstances and seek diverse solutions to these challenges. Superintendents should effectively communicate their suggestions and alternatives to enhance productivity within their teams.

Managers are tasked with selecting the most advantageous options from a range of possibilities, clarifying ambiguities, and making swift decisions when urgent situations arise. Managers must be capable of gathering information efficiently, ensuring they have a robust understanding of the problem at hand. This allows them to make well-informed choices within the confines of a limited timeframe, mitigating potential risks and optimizing outcomes.

DECISION MAKING In Depth

Gather Enough Information to Overcome Problems

Avoid quick fixes when confronted with issues. Develop strategic thinking traits such as curiosity, flexibility, future focus, positive outlook, and openness to new ideas. Delay decision-making when emotionally charged, ensuring a more balanced, rational approach once calmer. Continuously question the underlying causes of a problem, seek patterns, and evaluate multiple solutions. Reflect objectively on past decisions to recognize strengths and areas needing improvement.

Investigate into the Root of the Problem

Seek insights from those experienced in similar challenges or those affected by the problem to gain a deeper understanding of its root cause. Challenge yourself to gather additional data and stakeholder perspectives to confirm your assumptions. Spend significant time deeply analyzing a critical issue to uncover underlying factors and consult cross-functional insights to guide your understanding.

Find Different Ways to Solve Problems

Consider your company's strategies from the perspective of a supplier or customer to gain fresh insights. Employ tools like Six Sigma to better understand external issues affecting your operations. Furthermore, embracing fresh perspectives from new hires and a culture of open communication leads to innovative solutions that challenge the status quo. Viewing problems as processes allows for root cause analysis and potential process re-engineering, ultimately mitigating the impact of external factors. This comprehensive approach empowers companies to develop robust strategies that optimize supplier relationships, deliver superior customer value, and ensure long-term success.

Choose Wisely Between Different Options

Broaden your perspective by brainstorming with a diverse group to define the pros and cons of each potential solution. Balance pragmatism with strategic focus, favoring solutions that offer long-term benefits over those that are merely convenient in the short term. If uncertain about a decision, consider that the optimal solution often emerges after rejecting initial options. Seek additional inputs to enhance decision quality.

Decide, Even with Little Info or Data

Approach major decisions as a series of smaller ones, using feedback from each stage to refine subsequent choices. Request increased decision-making authority where practical to deepen your understanding of different business areas. Gain insights into decision-making principles from experts skilled at navigating complex choices and broaden your knowledge on unfamiliar topics to enhance your judgment. Recognize patterns from past experiences to speed up decision-making in urgent situations.

Finding Different Ways to Solve Problems

Regularly challenge the assumptions underlying your thinking, or "think outside the box." Present problems to a group and brainstorm possible causes to distinguish between symptoms and root causes. Engage in new activities to gain different perspectives that might spark innovative solutions. Step outside your comfort zone and engage in activities beyond your work domain, as exposure to new experiences can spark unexpected and valuable perspectives. Finally, ignite a spirit of healthy competition. Organize contests where advisory teams race against the clock to devise creative solutions. The pressure of a tight timeframe can foster innovative and effective solutions that propel your company forward.

MOTIVATION

Motivation in the context of leaders and employees refers to the internal or external factors that stimulate desire and energy in people to be continually interested and committed to a job and to exert persistent effort in attaining a goal. For leaders, motivation often stems from the drive to inspire and lead their teams effectively, achieving objectives while pushing for a positive and productive work environment. For employees, motivation can be driven by a variety of factors including personal fulfillment, recognition, financial incentives, professional growth, and a sense of belonging. Both intrinsic motivations, such as personal satisfaction and achievement, and extrinsic motivations, like rewards and recognition, play top roles in influencing the levels of engagement and output among team leaders and their team members.

Personal MOTIVATION

In a bustling postal service plant, the manager, Yanick, noticed a minor dip in team morale and efficiency as the peak holiday season approached. Everyone was running around and looks a bit overwhelmed. Recognizing the need for motivation, Yanick took a personal approach. One morning, he personally shook hands with each team member, wishing them happy holidays beforehand. As the manager was doing this, employees were looking at each other nodding agreeably at that gesture. This small, personal gesture not only lifted spirits but also stimulated a sense of appreciation and camaraderie among the team. To further enhance motivation, Yanick introduced a team-based incentive: if the team met their weekly targets for package sorting without errors, they would enjoy a prolonged break on Friday, extended by an extra 15 minutes. This extrinsic reward, combined with the intrinsic satisfaction from Yanick's personal acknowledgment, rejuvenated the team's spirit. As a result, the plant saw a noticeable improvement in both productivity and employee satisfaction, ensuring that the holiday rush was managed effectively and that team members felt valued and motivated.

Business MOTIVATION

A **supervisor's** role with motivation is pivotal in both upholding management decisions and inspiring their team. They should clearly communicate and support management's decisions, ensuring they are well-understood and integrated into the team's operations. It is paramount for supervisors to trust and demonstrate confidence in their team's abilities, which develops a positive and empowering work environment. This also includes showing enthusiasm for new projects, which can motivate the team and drive engagement. Supervisors should continually push for excellence, setting high standards and challenging the team to meet them. Acknowledging and rewarding these achievements not only boosts morale but also reinforces the behaviors that lead to success.

Superintendents play a key role also in aligning their team with the broader goals of the organization. They must endorse and reinforce management's decisions and objectives just like supervisors, making sure the team understands both the 'what' and the 'why' behind their tasks. By illuminating the path and purpose, superintendents keep their team motivated and focused on the organization's larger goals. They should propel team members to surpass established standards and to drive their own growth by taking initiative in their roles and on their own. This includes assigning specific, challenging tasks to individuals and providing the necessary support to achieve outstanding results, thus boosting a culture of self-motivation and continuous improvement.

Managers need to articulate a clear plan for their department that aligns with the company's overarching vision, providing clear and actionable guidance to ensure that everyone is moving in the same direction. They should challenge their teams to exceed their perceived limits and champion an environment where exceeding expectations is the norm. Recognizing individual contributions is essential for maintaining motivation and sense of accomplishment. Managers should aim to transform their departments into examples of success and innovation within the company. By assessing and utilizing each team member's unique strengths and weaknesses, managers can optimize task distribution, enhance productivity, and ensure that their team is well-positioned to succeed and set new records in performance.

MOTIVATION In DEPTH

I wanted this "Motivation in depth" to be in bullet points for several reasons:

A. <u>Clarity</u>: Bullet points ensure that the advice is clear and easy to note.
B. <u>Memorability</u>: This format helps you remember each piece of advice and revisit it easily.
C. <u>Highlighting</u>: You can highlight the points that resonate with you and apply them effectively.

By using bullet points, you can quickly identify the key takeaways and focus on the advice that matters most to you.

Championing Management Decisions

A. Ensure that you fully grasp the decisions and can articulate the process and benefits clearly. Present these decisions in your own words, thoroughly prepared to address any counterarguments. Avoid reading directly from a printed script.
B. Emphasize that the decision was "well-researched" to maximize productivity and "carefully considered" for safety and comprehensive benefits.
C. During your presentation, proactively discuss potential concerns your team may have about the decision and address any questions with an open mind.

Building Trust in Team Capabilities

A. Actively respond to real-time situations where a team member is performing well, providing immediate recognition and clarifying the benefits of their actions.

B. Prepare your team for potential pushback from their charges by encouraging proactive preparation and collaborative discussion of ideas.
C. Hold regular meetings to openly praise and thank your team for their individual efforts.
D. Show your trust by delegating decision-making or meeting leadership roles to team members in your absence.

Sustaining Personal Motivation and Optimism

A. Identify what drives your motivation and incorporate these motivators into your weekly routine as a reward.
B. Maintain a healthy work-life balance by managing your diet, sleep, and exercise, as these factors are critical for sustaining high energy levels and a positive work environment.
C. If feeling burnt out or limited by your current role, consider pursuing new challenges as a temporary shift to rejuvenate your interest and engagement.
D. Monitor and aim to reduce the frequency of negative or pessimistic remarks made during work to uphold a more positive atmosphere.

Driving Team Excellence

A. Set challenging and inspiring goals that encourage team members to venture into new areas and develop fresh skills.
B. At the beginning of the year, conduct a team meeting to establish performance standards, collaboratively defining what outstanding outcomes should look like.
C. Engage individually with team members to explore how each can contribute uniquely to achieving exceptional team results.
D. Maintain regular monitoring of departmental goals, recognizing and rewarding achievements, and customizing recognition plans to enhance various areas needing improvement (e.g., productivity awards, safety awards).

Aligning with Organizational Vision and Goals

A. Demonstrate commitment and vitality in all actions to advance your company's mission.
B. Reflect on the short- and long-term impacts of your decisions on others and align them closely with the organization's objectives and vision.
C. Ensure consistency between your words and actions, as your team will trust what they observe more than what they are told.
D. Regularly assess whether your approach aligns with the organization's vision, ensuring that your leadership effectively supports company-wide objectives.
E. Regularly evaluate your actions for consistency, particularly in making tough decisions, to ensure fairness and maintain leadership integrity.
F. Embrace and champion the adoption of new methodologies and technologies within the company, aiding your team in transitioning away from outdated practices and mindsets.

Fostering Self-Driven Efforts in Individuals

A. Dedicate time to build relationships within the organization and understand the needs of others. This network will be beneficial when you require assistance or collaboration.
B. Recognize and align the priorities of others with your own, which can mutually enhance your efforts towards achieving set goals and aspirations.
C. Give recognition where it's deserved to inspire a culture of appreciation and reciprocity among team members.
D. Seek a mentor who can provide guidance on your professional demeanor and motivations, helping you refine how you are perceived by others.
E. Form a trusted circle of colleagues or friends who can offer honest feedback on your management style, ensuring you stay aligned with your goals.

Select Capable Individuals to Innovate Solutions

A. Establish a feedback system to capture insights from staff and peers, remaining open to and flexible with new ideas that could significantly benefit operations.
B. Create an environment conducive to learning and adaptability, acknowledging that taking risks is part of growth and can lead to both successes and failures.
C. Review your own work habits to ensure you are utilizing your time and resources effectively, setting a positive example for your team.
D. Building a Trust-Based Platform for Success. Remember, trust is reciprocal; demonstrate trust in others to encourage a trusting atmosphere within your team.
E. Encourage your team to familiarize themselves with and embrace the company's strategic objectives and core values, addressing any misalignments that could affect daily operations.
F. Support team members even when errors occur, enhancing your credibility and reinforcing trust.

DEVELOP YOUR TEAM

Developing your team is vital, not only for boosting current productivity and efficiency but also for ensuring the long-term vitality and competitiveness of your entire organization. Well-developed teams are more adaptable, innovative, and capable of meeting the challenges of a rapidly changing business environment. Through continuous professional development, team members enhance their skills and knowledge, which directly translates into improved performance and efficiency. Moreover, teams that are regularly developed tend to have higher levels of job satisfaction and engagement, which are linked to lower turnover rates. This stability allows for the preservation of institutional knowledge and helps in building a more cohesive and dedicated workforce. In essence, the importance of developing your team cannot be overstated—it is a fundamental aspect that impacts not just the operational capabilities of the team but also its morale and long-term viability.

A **supervisor** is integral to the professional development of their team by offering constructive feedback tailored to individual strengths and areas for improvement. They have a keen understanding of each team member's capabilities and developmental needs, which allows them to recommend specific activities that help with growth. Supervisors play a supportive role, especially when employees take on new challenges or make mistakes, offering encouragement and emphasizing learning from these experiences. This supportive approach not only builds a resilient team but also creates an environment where continuous improvement is valued and encouraged.

Superintendents enhance team development through hands-on, real-time coaching, utilizing their own experiences and expertise as a learning resource for others. They hold team leaders accountable for the development of their staff, ensuring that growth and learning are consistent and aligned with organizational goals. Superintendents assist in identifying and prioritizing development objectives for their teams and make strategic placement and reward decisions that recognize individual performance and potential.

They also give team members the freedom to complete tasks in a way that suits their unique skills, with a sense of autonomy and confidence in their professional roles.

Managers are pivotal in shaping the future leadership of the organization by identifying and nurturing talent, creating pools of capable individuals ready to step into key roles. They address underperformance constructively, turning potential setbacks into learning opportunities that contribute to personal and professional growth. Managers work for an organizational culture that values the sharing of knowledge and expertise, facilitating a free flow of learning across all levels of the company. By strategically shaping roles and assignments, managers ensure that these are aligned with the developmental needs of their staff, leveraging individual strengths to maximize both personal and organizational success.

DEVELOP YOUR TEAM In DEPTH

Delivering Constructive Feedback Effectively

Avoid saving feedback for an annual review. Providing feedback soon after relevant events allows individuals to better understand the feedback in relation to specific situations. This approach not only makes the feedback more actionable but also builds trust, as employees see that feedback is aimed at continuous improvement rather than criticism at year-end. Employees are often adept at picking up on unspoken negativity from their bosses. This can be incredibly demotivating, especially when it leads to year-end surprises in evaluations. When a boss harbors unspoken negativity, it creates a tense and uncertain work environment. Employees, sensing this, may become anxious, disengaged, and minimize their effort in anticipation of potential criticism. This not only hurts morale but also hinders productivity.

Prepare for feedback sessions by gathering specific examples that highlight both strengths and areas needing development, ensuring that the feedback is based on real performance.

Be straightforward in your feedback discussions, being honest about your observations and the outcomes of their actions. Always recognize and appreciate when employees exhibit desirable behaviors, as this reinforces good practices and motivates continued good performance.

Sharing Experience and Expertise

Make yourself available to team members seeking guidance and share insights from your own experiences about what strategies have been effective. While offering advice, ensure that you respect their autonomy in decision-making. Encourage your leaders and team members to enhance their coaching and mentoring skills by taking on roles such as coaching someone from outside their immediate team, which can enrich their experience. Utilize experienced team members to help new members integrate into a team of a supportive culture. Share your own professional successes and setbacks openly to provide real-world learning opportunities, helping the team understand the value of learning from both successes and failures.

Understanding and Supporting Team Development

Conduct one-on-one discussions with each team member to gain a deeper understanding of their individual strengths, weaknesses, career aspirations, and motivations. This personalized approach helps in crafting development plans that are truly effective. Collect feedback from various sources, including peers and other internal stakeholders, to get a more complete picture of an employee's performance and areas for development. Motivate your team members to seek feedback from their peers, which can serve as valuable input for their personal development plans. Provide opportunities for team members to utilize their strengths and focus on improving their weaknesses. Employees are generally more engaged and motivated when they can enhance skills in which they are already proficient while also addressing developmental needs.

Recommending Development Activities to Others

To advance professional growth within your team, commit to implementing two or three specific development actions for each member, ensuring that these actions are specific, measurable, achievable, relevant, and time-bound (SMART). Keep in mind that the majority of development (70%) occurs through on-the-job experiences. Complement these experiences with feedback and coaching, which should constitute about 20% of the development process, while the remaining 10% can involve more formal training methods such as reading, tutor-led programs, and online courses. Additionally, look for opportunities outside your own organization, such as project participation, rotational assignments, and site visits, which can provide valuable new skills and experiences. If behavioral change is a goal for any team member, encourage them to keep a record of the times they exhibit the desired behavior, reviewing progress together at set intervals.

Providing Support and Encouragement for Developmental Risks

Encourage an open environment where team members feel safe to discuss mistakes and unsuccessful attempts at new approaches or behaviors. Help them analyze these situations to understand what didn't work and how they might adjust their actions in future attempts. It's essential for team members to take accountability for both successes and failures to support a learning culture; this means moving away from blaming others when things go wrong. Additionally, encourage peer learning by pairing team members with others who possess the skills or knowledge they need to develop, thereby enhancing the collective expertise within your team.

Delivering Effective Real-Time Coaching

To improve your coaching abilities, observe and meet with individuals who excel in coaching and consider incorporating their techniques into your own style. Personalize your coaching approach based on the unique needs and personalities of each team member.

This might mean providing reassurance to one employee while challenging another to push beyond their comfort zone. It is also crucial to solicit regular feedback from those you are coaching. Ask them what aspects of your coaching are helpful, what could be improved, and what should be discontinued to better support their learning and development. This feedback loop not only helps you refine your coaching methods but also makes the learning process more effective and tailored for everyone.

Holding Others Accountable for Developing Their Teams

As a manager or as a superintendent, and to ensure that leaders within your organization are actively developing their teams, work with them to set SMART (Specific, Measurable, Achievable, Realistic, and Time-bound) annual objectives aimed at enhancing the skill and competence levels of their members. Lead by example by holding regular performance review meetings with each of your leaders, discussing how they are improving their own skills and encouraging them to engage in similar practices with their teams. Additionally, conduct feedback meetings with employees who report to your leaders to gauge their perceptions on their personal development progress. Establish a set of standard people development metrics for your organization and require managers to report their progress on these metrics quarterly, using a color-coded system (green for on track, yellow for at risk, and red for behind) to easily identify the status of each goal.

Developing Successors and Talent Pools

Begin by identifying leadership talent early, adopting a long-term, 3–5-year view of your talent pipeline to ensure young talent is receiving the necessary structured development to join the succession pool. Collaborate with leaders across the organization to help successors develop robust business acumen and a comprehensive understanding of the organization. Make sure that high-potential individuals gain experience outside of your specific business line and take into account potential when recruiting talent from outside, aiming to attract individuals who could be future leaders, not just those who meet the immediate job requirements. Develop relationships with talent outside your business line and include them in your succession plans. Support a collaborative approach across the organization to develop talent, identifying leadership roles that benefit the organization as a whole.

Handling Underperformance Productively

When addressing underperformance, work closely with the individual to understand the root causes, whether they are motivational, skill-based, or related to misunderstandings of job expectations. Agree on a realistic development plan to address identified performance gaps, ensuring the plan includes clear outcomes, timelines, and support mechanisms. Regularly review this plan with the employee or leader to monitor progress and ensure the organization is providing the necessary support. Maintain a constructive working relationship throughout this process, encouraging open dialogue about performance issues, which is essential for effective resolution. Remember, it is unfair to both the individual and the organization not to address performance issues, as unrecognized developmental gaps can hinder both personal and organizational growth.

Promoting Sharing of Expertise

To enhance organizational learning and expertise sharing, actively network with peers across the company to uncover common interests and potential areas for resource and knowledge sharing. Propel your team members to participate in internal training programs where they can interact with peers from different departments. Upon their return, have them share knowledge they have gained about other functions or business areas with the rest of the team. Additionally, nominate team members for cross-departmental projects that offer opportunities for collaboration and learning. These initiatives not only enrich individual knowledge but also strengthen interdepartmental connections and build a culture of continuous learning within the company.

Shaping Roles and Assignments to Develop Capabilities

Be mindful of the potential for roles to become stale; research suggests that individuals may need new challenges after 3-5 years in the same position. To keep team members engaged and learning, assign them stretch objectives, advocate for role-swapping with peers, or involve them in managing new projects. Wherever possible, integrate discussions about business plans with team and personal development conversations, identifying new developmental opportunities as business objectives evolve. Focus on leveraging and enhancing team members' strengths rather than solely addressing weaknesses. Consider facilitating lateral moves or assigning team members to different functional areas or business units. Such broadened experiences can spur innovation and provide fresh perspectives on their roles, contributing to both personal growth and organizational development.

SHOW ADAPTIBILITY, MANAGE STRESS!

As you ascend to higher positions within an organization, the ambiguity of your responsibilities increases. To navigate this successfully, leaders must refine their ability to make well-informed decisions swiftly and effectively, often with limited information and without historical precedents to guide them. Furthermore, it is essential for leaders to understand that their current knowledge may not suffice to tackle future challenges. Learning from the lessons offered by setbacks and failures is very important, as these experiences provide valuable opportunities for learning, adaptation, and growth. Effective management of one's reactions to unfavorable situations, is fundamental for leading through uncertain times and are indispensable to achieving leadership success.

Working Under STRESS

A good leader thrives in environments of stress and uncertainty by employing constructive strategies and methods. When overwhelmed, consider breaking sizable projects into manageable, progressive steps, allowing for adaptive changes as conditions evolve. For those inclined towards perfectionism, it's required to strike a balance between deliberation and action, setting goals to reduce reliance on extensive data or to make minor decisions without any data at all. When faced with intimidating challenges, translating them into a visual representation can be beneficial; utilize a whiteboard to diagram the process flow or construct a narrative for the issue at hand. It's also important to discern and discard non-essential tasks as not all demand equal urgency. Furthermore, to assist your team in navigating ambiguity, effectively communicate the reasons behind changes along with the methods and expected outcomes. This approach not only keeps the focus on long-term goals but also satisfies the team's need to see immediate progress, promoting a cohesive and motivated work environment.

Adjusting Your Needs

Efficiently adjusts to evolving needs, circumstances, priorities, and opportunities by actively broadening experiences through engaging in diverse activities beyond the workplace. Explore new sports, hobbies, meet different people, and dine at unfamiliar restaurants without prior research to foster adaptability. For those who struggle with organization or find little time to adjust as situations shift, it's imperative to identify essential priorities and allocate time each week to advance these key projects. When the nature of a problem remains unclear, dedicate time to dissect the root cause to avoid perpetually treating mere symptoms. Enhance understanding of priorities by asking more questions before initiating actions.

Working with Failures and Mistakes with Open Mind

Always, addresses personal failures and mistakes constructively. Acknowledge errors promptly to obtain a trustful atmosphere, encouraging transparency among peers. Seek assistance in pinpointing alternative approaches for future situations to avert repeated mistakes. Determine if a mistake signals a learning gap; collaborate with your supervisor to find a subject matter expert who can provide necessary knowledge or skills. This proactive approach not only mitigates future errors but also enhances personal and professional growth.

Actively Pursues Knowledge and Skill Enhancement

Proactively seeks opportunities for personal and professional growth by stepping outside of one's expertise to teach unfamiliar subjects, thereby embracing the learning curve of a novice. Challenge yourself to step out of your comfort zone by taking calculated risks in both personal and professional life. Experiment with new roles, such as acting as a spokesperson in high-stakes situations, or by adopting behavioral approaches that are contrary to your usual methods—for instance, coaching rather than instructing, delegating instead of solving problems directly. These experiences alter outcomes and contribute to your personal development.

Demonstrates Insight into Personal Strengths and Development Areas

To enhance understanding of personal capabilities and areas needing improvement, actively seek feedback from colleagues and supervisors. Requesting both positive and constructive feedback can sharpen your self-awareness and increase your effectiveness. Consider asking for confidential 360° feedback to gain a comprehensive view of your strengths and weaknesses. <u>Be aware that success can breed</u> arrogance, which may block career advancement and discourage others from providing valuable feedback. Persistent in your requests for information to show true commitment to self-improvement. Recognize that defensiveness is a barrier to self-knowledge; acquiring strong listening skills is beneficial. Identify key areas for development, create a targeted action plan, and continuously review and adapt your strategy based on feedback to ensure you are making meaningful progress.

Embraces Feedback with Openness and Without Defensiveness

Actively work to recognize and manage your emotional triggers by documenting instances where you lost composure to identify patterns and underlying causes. Develop strategies for better mental and physical reactions to these triggers, aiming to decrease such occurrences. Practice pausing before responding impulsively; for instance, count to ten or jot down notes to allow time for a more considered reply. Observe and learn from defensiveness and anger in others, noticing if they often use prescriptive language like 'should' or 'must,' and reflect on whether you do the same. When receiving constructive feedback, perceive it as addressing the issue at hand rather than as a personal critique, and spend adequate time understanding the problem to improve future handling of similar situations. A truly effective leader welcomes feedback with an open mind, avoiding defensiveness. This fosters a learning environment and earns you amazement, admiration, and respect from your subordinates.

Demonstrates Readiness for New Challenges and Risks for Growth

Prepare to navigate uncertain environments by routinely engaging in activities that disrupt your normal patterns or push you out of your comfort zone. Actively seek roles requiring adaptability and be vigilant in spotting both opportunities and potential threats within your industry by analyzing trends and scenarios in business publications. Upon facing changes or shifting priorities, refrain from immediate reactions; instead, gather more information to inform your responses. View these changes as chances to employ creative thinking and assert your capability to devise solutions to emerging challenges, reinforcing your readiness to tackle obstacles innovatively.

Demonstrates Adaptability Across Diverse Scenarios

Take deliberate steps to evaluate your current circumstances and decide if they necessitate alterations in your routines, assumptions, or relationships. Reflect on similar past experiences to better plan and manage potential changes. Conduct a thorough self-assessment to understand your typical reactions to change, identifying strengths to leverage and situations that induce stress. Determine strategies to handle these stressors more effectively in the future. Also, consider your support network; identify individuals who can offer guidance or support in adapting to new situations. Focus your efforts on your most challenging tasks, identifying what can be delegated or postponed managing your workload effectively.

Maintains Positivity and Humor in Adverse Conditions

Seek an optimistic mindset, anticipating positive outcomes to enhance your likelihood of success, as attitudes often influence outcomes. Direct your energy toward finding alternative solutions rather than dwelling on obstacles. View difficult challenges as opportunities for learning, recognizing that each scenario offers valuable lessons.

Concentrate on the facts of the situation rather than the feared consequences, assessing whether the issue requires a minor adjustment or a more significant change. Manage your attitude proactively; embracing lessons from setbacks can significantly improve your future success. Additionally, prioritize your physical and emotional well-being to sustain high energy levels and maintain a positive perspective, essential for navigating tough situations with humor and resilience.

Adapts Leadership Style to Meet Situational Demands

Start by gaining a deep understanding of yourself, which can serve as a foundation for understanding others. Engage in a 360° feedback process, soliciting honest assessments from others about your strengths and weaknesses, and use this information as a baseline to gauge others' behaviors. Observe and study your colleagues' behaviors, strengths, weaknesses, and preferences to better predict their reactions in various situations. When assigning tasks, consider the individual's knowledge and experience level, adjusting your leadership approach based on the task's difficulty and the person's capabilities. Recognize that every individual possesses both positive and negative traits; as a leader, provide constructive feedback, make critical decisions about promotions, or even dismissals. Tailor your leadership style to suit the nature of the conversation and the message being conveyed. Always remain open to new information and be willing to revise your opinions about people.

Responds Resourcefully to New Challenges and Demands

When facing difficulties in accomplishing tasks, explore various approaches to achieve the desired outcomes, preparing to adapt as challenges arise. Don't take resistance personally; maintain objectivity, articulate the business rationale clearly, and intensify efforts to listen and respond to objections as you approach your goal. Prepare wisely to present a compelling case, utilizing precise language and rehearsing responses to potential tough questions to convincingly communicate your conviction in your proposals.

Consider both formal and informal organizational structures to navigate and accomplish goals, and when new priorities emerge, realign your team's focus and resources to ensure key objectives are met.

Exhibits Flexibility and Resilience Under Pressure

Seek out colleagues who have effectively managed adversity and learn from their experiences, strategies, and outcomes. Exercise patience during times of constraint and adversity, opting to listen and observe rather than immediately taking assertive action. Acknowledge that not all projects must be completed to 100% to fulfill their purposes; understanding when to cease pushing for full completion can optimize results and conserve resources. Maintain a focus on the broader picture, balancing demanding tasks with less challenging activities and allowing time for recuperation by engaging in areas within your comfort zone where outcomes are more predictable and manageable.

Navigates Organizational Politics Like an Expert

To adeptly handle the political dynamics within your organization, start by thoroughly understanding the political rules and landscape. Pay close attention to who holds decision-making power, the processes by which decisions are made, and the methods used for resource allocation. Maintain a broad network of relationships across the organization, which can provide insights into the internal political climate that aren't typically available through official channels. Approach initial proposals with caution, allowing flexibility for adjustments and adaptations by others; this approach can prevent potential conflicts that often arise from presenting rigid or extreme positions early on.

Being politically astute also requires a keen sensitivity to interpersonal dynamics. Develop the ability to read and anticipate people's reactions, enhancing your effectiveness in navigating and influencing within the complex social structures of your workplace.

Part III: Enhancing Communication and Relationships

> *The single biggest problem in communication is the illusion that it has taken place.*
>
> George Bernard Shaw

COMMUNICATION SKILLS

It's no secret that effective communication is the cornerstone of a thriving organization. Expressing ideas with clarity and confidence, actively listening to understand, and tailoring your message to diverse audiences are the hallmarks of a strong communicator. While everyone recognizes its importance, many struggle with putting it into practice. Savvy leaders prioritize fostering an environment where communication is not just open and frequent, but also targeted and actively encouraged. While cultivating such a culture may present challenges, the rewards are undeniable: a motivated workforce, streamlined operations, smoother change management, and a constant spark of innovation.

Moreover, clear communication will definitely minimize misunderstandings, boosts efficiency, and strengthens relationships with colleagues and clients alike. This commitment to robust communication channels is the bedrock of an organization's success and adaptability in today's dynamic world.

COMMUNICATION SKILLS In DEPTH

Enhancing Communication through Active Engagement and Empathy

Active listening demands nerves of steel, as it requires holding yourself back from speaking while navigating emotional conversations or acknowledging the speaker's need to vent before offering solutions. To practice active listening, avoid interrupting and maintain positive, encouraging body language, knowing that this temporary silence is a powerful tool, fostering trust and creating space for deeper understanding because It's during these moments that true connection is built, paving the way for more effective problem-solving and a more positive work environment.

Once they have finished speaking, provide your feedback thoughtfully. Keep a record of situations where you attempted to listen attentively, noting what you did well and areas for improvement. In the future, pay special attention to non-verbal cues. Try to understand the emotions being communicated and confirm your interpretations with the speaker before responding. Assess your progress in understanding others and practice patience. <u>Avoid cutting others off, suggesting words during their pauses, or finishing their sentences</u>. Remain open and avoid dismissive responses like "Yes, I know that" or "I know what you're going to say." Strive to listen impartially to everyone, regardless of their seniority, race, or gender. If time is short, reschedule discussions rather than compromising the quality of the dialogue. When faced with negative feedback, focus on understanding the message, remain calm, and ask clarifying questions. Ensure that you are truly listening rather than judging, particularly with individuals you may not respect. Keep an open mind, ask questions to allow others to express their points fully, and withhold judgments until you have had adequate time to reflect on the conversation. By approaching communication with this mindset, you'll transform yourself from a listener to a true leader and collaborator, fostering a culture of shared success.

Encouraging Contributions from Every Voice in the Room

To achieve a balance between talking and listening, consider inviting a peer to observe you during a meeting and provide feedback on how well you manage this equilibrium. Start each interaction with a clear statement of its purpose; this will guide how much you speak versus listen. For example, if the goal is to share information, you might dominate the conversation, but if you're seeking opinions or feedback, ensure you give others ample time to express themselves. It's important not to focus solely on the loudest or most confident participants. Actively encourage those who typically listen more to share their thoughts and contribute to the discussion. This approach creates a more inclusive environment where everyone feels valued and can participate meaningfully.

Adapting Communication Styles for <u>Understanding and Trust</u>

Effective communication requires sensitivity to your audience's needs. Tailor your timing, tone, style, and tactics based on a deep understanding of what will resonate in each specific situation. Always clarify the purpose of your discussions, ensuring that people grasp the subject and context of your consultations. If you struggle to articulate your thoughts clearly, you may find it challenging to gather useful feedback. Be forthright about what you know and what you don't. If you encounter questions that you can't answer, commit to investigating further and providing a response later—this honesty deepens trust and strengthens professional relationships. When possible, opt for face-to-face interactions, especially when conveying complex or potentially negative information. Nonverbal cues and a genuine demeanor can significantly enhance the clarity and impact of your message. This approach allows for direct and open sharing of viewpoints, which is essential for effective communication and mutual understanding.

Strategic Communication Practices for Upper Leaders

To ensure that all critical stakeholders are appropriately informed, leaders should adopt a structured approach to communication. Organize regular update meetings to exchange "urgent and important "information, and actively inquire about the specific needs of your team and other stakeholders regarding the information they require and their preferred formats. <u>Promptly respond to emails and other correspondences</u>, fulfilling your commitments reliably to build credibility and trust. Be transparent about what information you can share and clearly communicate any limitations to avoid misunderstandings. Make sure to identify all relevant parties early in the process and engage with them frequently to prevent any resistance that might arise from feeling excluded. This proactive and open approach to communication supports the creation of a transparent and trusting environment, facilitating smoother operations and more effective leadership.

Strategies for Encouraging Participation and Valuing Contributions

Encourage the generation of new ideas by organizing brainstorming sessions that adhere to best practices, ensuring that every team member has the chance to contribute without immediate judgment or dismissal. Such inclusivity can often lead to surprising insights from unexpected sources. Create an environment conducive to creativity by minimizing distractions and interruptions during these sessions, and by limiting frequent progress checks that might hinder free thinking. Actively implement the most promising ideas within your organization to promote an ongoing culture of innovation and acknowledge the contributors effectively to motivate continual engagement and idea generation. Recognition should extend beyond the immediate team, emphasizing the value of these contributions across the broader organization. Integrate stakeholder feedback early in the project process, setting clear goals for outcomes and deliverables while maintaining flexibility in the approach to encourage creative solutions.

Adopt a neutral attitude towards failure and criticism; recognize that innovation inherently involves risks and learning from mistakes. Support your team in these endeavors, encouraging them to analyze setbacks constructively rather than fear them. Finally, temper expectations about achieving perfection on the first attempt, as this mindset can stifle innovation and perpetuate conventional methods. By valuing process and progress, you cultivate a forward-thinking environment where creativity thrives.

Techniques for Clarifying Understanding and Offering Feedback Respectfully

Effective communicators understand the importance of truly listening to others rather than simply preparing to respond. To avoid the appearance of merely "reloading" while someone else is speaking, take a moment after they finish to paraphrase their points. This not only checks your understanding but also minimizes the chance of miscommunication and demonstrates active listening.
If clarity is still needed, don't hesitate to ask further questions. By asking questions to clarify, you signal to the speaker that you are genuinely engaged and striving to fully grasp their perspective.

When expressing your own reactions and opinions, begin interactions with a moment of rapport-building. Discussing a non-business topic at the start of a meeting like the weather or the current events, can create a more relaxed atmosphere, making it easier for others to receive your feedback later without feeling intimidated. Reflect on any feedback you receive about your interaction style—whether you come across as too forceful, or perhaps not engaging enough. Adjust your communication approach based on your audience's feedback and your own observations about what methods yield the best results in various situations.

Are they experts in the field, or do they need foundational information? Technical jargon might fly with colleagues, but a client presentation might require simpler terms as you will see in the next subject. This sensitivity and adaptability in your communications can create a more open and constructive exchange of ideas.

Adapting Messages for Comprehensive Reach and Inclusivity

To communicate effectively across various levels within an organization, it is essential to consider the specific characteristics and knowledge base of your audience. Determine what they already know and what you need them to do, then tailor your writing and presentations to meet these requirements. Regularly engage with your staff to understand the information they find most useful and reciprocate by sharing your expectations of the information you need from them. Employ multiple communication methods to ensure your message reaches diverse groups while maintaining a consistent underlying message throughout. Adjust your writing style and the level of detail according to the intended audience, ensuring the core message remains consistent across all communications. Engage with individuals from different companies or cultures to grasp communication style variances and apply these insights to enhance your communication strategy. Include representatives from key stakeholder groups in the message development process to ensure the tone, content, and level of detail are appropriate for each segment of your audience.

Building an Inclusive and Collaborative Work Environment

Structure staff meetings to democratize information flow, inviting various team members to provide updates and share insights, rather than positioning yourself as the sole source of information. Adapt an atmosphere where providing honest feedback, including potentially unfavorable news, is appreciated rather than penalized. **Express gratitude to those who display the courage to deliver critical updates,** emphasizing the value of their honesty. Focus intently on the ideas, thoughts, and feelings expressed by others during conversations, ensuring they feel heard and respected. By prioritizing listening over responding, you demonstrate that their viewpoints are important. Acknowledge and integrate the contributions of others into your decision-making process, showcasing that their input is not only heard but acted upon, thereby cultivating a culture of respect and collaboration.

Strategies for Effective Information Exchange

To ensure the clarity and impact of your written communications for example, it is advisable to first save drafts of important emails and documents before sending them. Allow yourself a few hours to revisit these drafts, providing a fresh perspective to identify any errors and refine your message. For particularly critical communications, consider having them reviewed by a trusted colleague for both clarity and impact. Engage with your team and colleagues to determine the types of information they find valuable and establish a mutual understanding of the communication both parties' desire.

Your Big Presentation

As a team leader preparing for a presentation that compares current data with last year's figures and forecasts future trends, it's requisite to structure your presentation clearly. Begin by outlining your objectives that align with your organization's strategic goals.

Use well-designed charts and graphs to visually represent past performance and future projections. Be prepared to answer spontaneous questions from upper management during the presentation. Deepen your understanding of the data to respond confidently and concisely. Remember, prior to delivering a formal presentation, rehearse thoroughly to refine your delivery and seek feedback from colleagues to ensure your message is both effective and persuasive.

At the end, effective communication is fundamental to the success of any organization. It enables clear understanding, encourages collaboration, and builds trust among team members across all levels. By ensuring that messages are tailored and responsive to the needs of diverse audiences, leaders can facilitate better decision-making, enhance organizational alignment, and drive positive outcomes. Moreover, respectful and inclusive communication practices strengthen relationships and empower individuals, highlighting the profound impact that skillful communication has on achieving sustained organizational success and a harmonious work environment.

BUILDING AND MAINTAINING RELATIONSHIPS

Effective leaders recognize the importance of garnering support, cooperation, and goodwill from their superiors, peers, and teams to achieve their objectives. Skilled in navigating both the formal and informal networks within their organization, they adeptly manage to meet the diverse needs of various internal and external stakeholders. By seamlessly switching gears to address different requirements, these leaders foster a collaborative environment where productivity thrives. Ultimately, the most successful leaders are those whom others eagerly want to work with and for, as they consistently create positive, results-driven workspaces. And all of that is possible by: Maintaining Relationships.

Mastering the Art of Rapport

Effective rapport-building is a core skill for successful interactions, involving a mutual exchange of information and personal insights. Those adept at creating rapport openly share their thoughts on business issues and encourage others to respond, enhancing workplace communication and broadening perspectives. By revealing personal details not necessarily related to work, leaders can stimulate a sense of trust and inclusivity among their team members. It's important to treat colleagues as individuals and make an effort to remember personal details such as their interests or family lives, which can serve as common ground in conversations beyond the immediate business agenda. Observing body language can also provide insights into how well your attempts to connect are being received. <u>If you notice signs of discomfort or disengagement, such as avoiding eye contact or hesitating in speech, it may be an indication to adjust your approach.</u>

Non-verbal cues play a critical role in communication; maintaining eye contact, nodding in agreement, and adopting an open posture can significantly enhance how your engagement is perceived. Strive to keep your tone even and relaxed and be mindful not to overwhelm with overly rapid or forceful speech.

Avoid behaviors that might suggest disinterest, <u>such as checking your phone or multitasking during conversations</u>. For those who are shy, practicing casual conversations with strangers outside of work can boost confidence. Observing and emulating how confidently people initiate and maintain communications can be highly beneficial. Engaging in low-risk social interactions can gradually build your comfort and effectiveness in more challenging or professional scenarios, enhancing your ability to establish rapport across a range of situations.

Cultivating Respect and Inclusion Across Diverse Work Environments

In a global, multicultural cities all over the world, respecting and understanding people from different cultural, personal, and professional backgrounds is essential. One practical approach to bridge cultural divides is to engage with colleagues in everyday settings, such as during lunch or after work events. These moments provide valuable opportunities for exchanging views and deepening understanding across cultural lines. It's important to see each person as an individual, avoiding stereotypes and challenging your own preconceptions to ensure fair and consistent treatment. Participating in teams or activities where you are in the minority can offer insightful perspectives into the experiences of others and help stimulate empathy. Identifying and addressing any personal discomfort in such settings can lead to greater inclusivity and understanding. <u>Additionally, acknowledging the linguistic diversity of the workforce, especially in environments where many may not speak the country's language as a first language</u>, is crucial. Listening actively to all contributions and adapting your communication style to meet various needs shows respect and facilitates better teamwork.

Leaders should adapt their management styles not only to cultural backgrounds but also to individual personality types and experience levels. This tailored approach can enhance team dynamics and improve overall productivity by ensuring that all team members feel valued and respected.

This commitment to inclusivity not only enriches the workplace culture but also drives innovation and collaboration by harnessing the diverse strengths and perspectives of all employees.

Expressing Viewpoints Constructively

Expressing your viewpoint tactfully is needed to avoid unnecessary conflicts that can derail productive discussions. The choice of language, timing, and tone plays a significant role in how messages are received and interpreted. To prevent conflict, ensure your language is not offensive, avoid raising your voice, and use a neutral tone that allows others to maintain dignity. Focus your words on the issue at hand rather than the person involved, clearly describing the problem and its impacts without assigning blame. Starting conversations on common ground can set a positive tone and boost a cooperative relationship. Respect for others' positions is essential in creating a harmonious environment. To enhance your communication skills, keep track of instances where you refrain from interrupting others, allowing them to complete their thoughts, and set goals to improve this behavior over time.

Additionally, adopt a question-based approach to conversations to encourage dialogue and reduce the perception of confrontation. For instance, instead of reminding someone abruptly about a deadline like "Don't forget the "Productivity" report is due on Monday morning," ask "How is the "Productivity" report coming along?" This method opens up communication, making interactions more collaborative and less adversarial.

Navigating Challenges and Conflicts Constructively

Maintaining positive relationships, even in difficult interpersonal situations, requires self-awareness and deliberate action. Begin by identifying your triggers—those hot buttons that provoke emotional reactions. Reflect on recent instances where you lost control of your temper and try to understand why these specific issues affected you so intensely. Work on envisioning and practicing more appropriate responses, aiming to reduce the frequency of your reactive outbursts.

When faced with a trigger, practice pausing before reacting to consider a more constructive behavior. Strive to respond objectively, focusing on describing issues rather than attacking the person involved. Active listening plays a crucial role; make a concerted effort to understand the other person's perspective, allowing them ample space to articulate their feelings and opinions. Emphasize your interest in their views and express confidence in finding a mutually acceptable solution. Conclude interactions on a friendly note by shifting the conversation to non-work-related topics, which can help strengthen the relationship further.

To prevent conflicts from escalating, cultivate a healthy work-life balance and engage in physical activities, as exercise can be an effective way to manage stress and control temper. When conflicts do arise, <u>maintain objectivity and remember that resistance is typically more about the situation than it is personal</u>. Stay focused on the business objectives and listen to feedback to respond appropriately. Always anchor discussions in facts and shared goals. By putting yourself in the other person's shoes, you can gain insights into their reactions and foster a more empathetic understanding. Learning from how peers handle similar challenges and applying viable strategies can also aid in staying resilient and positive, ensuring you rebound from conflicts without harboring grudges.

Moving Beyond Conflict Without Resentment

To effectively rebound from conflict and avoid holding grudges, it's necessary to maintain objectivity and remember that resistance in the workplace is usually not personal but a normal aspect of professional interactions. Focus on the business case and consistently steer discussions back to the facts and shared objectives. Listening to feedback and responding thoughtfully is essential; it demonstrates a commitment to understanding and addressing underlying issues. Recognizing that conflicts often arise from passion for one's work can help you empathize with others.
Before reacting defensively, try to see the situation from the other person's perspective, considering how they might feel and why they reacted as they did.

Additionally, engage with colleagues to gain insights into how they handle similar situations and remain positive despite challenges. Learning from others' experiences and adopting strategies that resonate with your circumstances can be invaluable. This approach not only helps in resolving current conflicts but also in preventing future misunderstandings and fostering a more cooperative and supportive workplace environment.

Focusing on Solutions, Not Personalities

Resolving conflicts constructively is central to building cooperative relationships and requires adopting a partnership approach. This involves increasing the fairness of dialogues, not aiming to win every argument but instead seeking common ground that reflects mutual interests. It's useful to concede on minor points and avoid rigid stances from the start. Showing respect for others' views and minimizing conflicts are crucial steps. When tensions rise, give the other party space to express their frustrations without interruption. Engage them with open-ended questions such as, "What change could enhance our collaboration?" or "How can I assist you effectively?" This allows them to vent, potentially reducing the intensity of their concerns as they speak.

Continuously negotiate by exploring what the other party needs and what you can offer outside the immediate conflict, facilitating a give-and-take dynamic. It's essential to understand and articulate the opposing viewpoint as accurately as the stakeholders do, showing you consider their perspective valid. Don't fixate on a single solution; instead, explore various options to resolve the issue. When faced with a challenge, avoid getting tunnel vision on a single answer. Brainstorm a variety of potential solutions, considering different angles and approaches. If you find yourself stuck, consult a trusted colleague who can provide an unbiased perspective and possibly suggest alternative solutions. This external input might also inspire you to reconsider your stance if it lacks sufficient support. Always be willing to adapt and brainstorm with your team for alternative strategies that achieve the desired outcomes, demonstrating flexibility and openness to different approaches in conflict resolution.

Leveraging Diversity Across Functions and Locations

Effective networking involves cultivating relationships not just within your own team or department but across various functions and locations, both inside and outside the organization. Initiate meetings with peers from different work units to discover how your teams can collaborate more efficiently. Implement their suggestions through structured plans, and consider including individuals from outside your work unit in your projects, either through temporary transfers or as part-time members of your core team. Further extend your network by leading a task force to address critical issues within your organization, involving diverse groups from different functions. Outside the organization, join professional groups to gain broader insights, coaching, and support. Engage with peers from vendor and customer organizations to understand their perspectives on shared challenges and explore opportunities for closer collaboration.

Navigating Organizational Politics and Stakeholder Interests

To prevent and resolve emerging conflicts effectively, engage with key stakeholders individually before significant meetings. This one-on-one dialogue allows you to explain your proposals clearly and understand their positions and concerns, fostering a mutual exploration of potential solutions. Early involvement of stakeholders in the solution-finding process helps them become advocates for the implementation of these solutions. It's also crucial to develop a keen understanding of your organization's political landscape by identifying key influencers and opinion leaders. By understanding who holds sway and who others listen to, you can tailor your communication strategies to resonate with these individuals, ensuring your message reaches the right ears. Recognizing that influence in decision-making may not always align with seniority can guide you in engaging the right people to support your initiatives, ensuring smoother project execution and organizational harmony.

Mediating Conflicts and Facilitating Agreement

As an effective mediator, your role is to facilitate consensus among groups with differing viewpoints, particularly on critical issues. Keep the dialogue ongoing and strive to resolve disputes at the earliest stages to prevent escalation. If discussions become heated, consider scheduling breaks to allow emotions to settle and prevent conversations from becoming personal or destructive. Establish clear rules for meetings upfront, such as staying objective, addressing issues directly, and maintaining a constructive approach. Refer back to these rules to keep discussions on track if participants stray. Utilize visual aids like a flip chart to outline shared interests and potential areas for compromise, which can visually reinforce the possibilities for agreement and minimize points of contention. In challenging situations, employing a third-party facilitator can provide an unbiased perspective to help maintain control of the meeting's agenda, offering a learning opportunity for observing effective negotiation techniques.

Valuing Diversity and Fostering Engagement Across the Organization

To support a culture where everyone feels valued and respected, start by clearly communicating the organization's values and expected behaviors during team meetings. Encourage the team to establish their own ground rules for behavior that align with these values. Ensure that every member has the opportunity to speak during meetings, actively soliciting input from those who may be less inclined to volunteer their thoughts.

Recognize and thank individuals who demonstrate positive behaviors that serve as role models in the team. Implement a metric to track diversity within critical functions or business areas, setting specific objectives related to this metric. Regularly discuss progress towards these diversity goals with your leaders, maintaining a focus on continuous improvement and inclusivity at all organizational levels.

At the end, effective relationship management is pivotal in both personal and professional settings, revolving around the principles of communication, respect, and empathy. To propel relationships, it's essential to actively listen, share openly, and value diverse perspectives. Maintaining a positive rapport requires understanding and addressing others' needs and viewpoints, establishing trust, and ensuring consistent and constructive interactions. By emphasizing fairness, inclusivity, and cooperation, and by managing conflicts thoughtfully, individuals can cultivate lasting connections that are mutually beneficial and supportive. This approach not only enhances interpersonal dynamics but also drives collective success in achieving common goals.

ENCOURAGING TEAMWORK

In today's complex environment, effective collaboration across various departments is essential. While individual accomplishments are notable, collective efforts often yield superior results. Leaders must therefore hone their skills in teamwork and cross-departmental collaboration. It is crucial for them to understand and facilitate the dynamics of team interactions to leverage the diverse talents and perspectives that each member brings. This collaborative approach not only amplifies individual strengths but also propels the entire organization towards greater innovation and success.

Valuing Contributions and Pursuing Teamwork Across Boundaries

To cultivate a vibrant and innovative workplace, it is essential to acknowledge and celebrate the contributions of team members. Leaders should ensure that recognition for good ideas and successful implementations cascades beyond their immediate work units. Actively promoting and adopting the best ideas from team members not only fosters creative thinking but also builds a culture where employees feel encouraged to appreciate each other openly. Organizing events to recognize team achievements can further reinforce this culture of gratitude and recognition.

Expanding collaboration beyond traditional departmental lines is another key strategy for enhancing organizational effectiveness. Leaders should seek opportunities to meet with peers from different departments to explore how teams can interoperate more seamlessly. Developing plans to integrate these suggestions and involving individuals from other departments in projects, whether through temporary assignments or part-time involvement, can significantly enhance project outcomes. Additionally, engaging with external stakeholders like vendors and customers to collaborate on mutually beneficial projects can open new avenues for innovation.

Allowing team members to participate in external projects not only helps in skill development and fostering a global mindset but also positions your team as a collaborative partner within and outside the organization.

Instilling Shared Values and Norms for Collective Success

To build team cohesiveness, it is essential to establish, communicate, and reinforce shared values and behavioral norms. Leaders should encourage their teams to set and adhere to clear ground rules that promote constructive interactions, such as not interrupting others, building on colleagues' ideas, arriving punctually at meetings, and holding each other accountable for results. Regular reminders of these rules during team meetings help maintain discipline and mutual respect.

Developing a common sense of direction is equally important. A unified mindset and a shared mission inspire high performance. Involving team members in defining collective goals, metrics, and success markers is critical. Setting and reviewing milestones allows the team to monitor their progress effectively. This structured approach not only clarifies expectations but also strengthens the team's dedication to their collective mission.

Ensuring Inclusivity and Awareness in Decision-Making

When leading a project, it's necessary to identify and involve all stakeholders who might be impacted by the project's outcomes. Engage these individuals or groups at relevant stages to ensure their perspectives and needs are considered, maintaining open and frequent communication throughout the project's lifecycle. Additionally, enhancing your team with people from outside your department, through temporary transfers or part-time roles, can provide fresh insights and foster cross-departmental collaboration. To fully understand the broader business context and enhance your project's relevance and effectiveness, consider visiting other locations or participating in their projects.

This not only builds a deeper understanding of different parts of the organization but also prepares you to better involve these areas in future initiatives. Always consider the potential impacts on suppliers and customers, and proactively communicate with them about any plans that may affect their operations. Their experiences with similar challenges may offer practical advice and support, ensuring your project not only succeeds internally but also aligns well with external partners' needs and expectations. This comprehensive approach to stakeholder engagement helps in making informed decisions and strengthens the project's overall success.

Mutual Support and Learning

To optimize team performance, it is essential to cultivate an environment where trust thrives, encouraging team members to explore and leverage their unique strengths and address developmental needs. By evaluating projects based on the skills required for successful execution and identifying any gaps, teams can implement targeted plans for skill enhancement. Social activities and celebrating achievements together also play a crucial role in building team cohesion, as these interactions deepen mutual understanding and improve collective efficiency.

Encouraging team members who do not usually collaborate to work together on projects can be an effective team-building strategy. By having team members articulate each person's unique contributions, everyone gains a clearer perspective of the diverse strengths within the team. This exercise helps in crafting a list that highlights both similarities and differences among team members, fostering appreciation of varied skills and experiences. Building a high-performing team revolves around rallying everyone around a shared goal, setting meaningful challenges, and providing the necessary autonomy and resources. Regularly acknowledging their contributions, maintaining an active interest in their tasks, establishing clear, measurable outcomes, and celebrating successes collectively are all strategies that enhance motivation and drive teams toward exceptional performance.

Influence and Cooperation Among Peers

To contribute effectively to group outcomes, it is imperative to develop your influencing skills. Begin by identifying how you can assist others in your team, as this often encourages reciprocal support. Invest time in understanding the perspectives of your colleagues, particularly those from whom you need support. Consider the impact of your work on them and if it's negative, explore ways to mitigate this, such as volunteering your staff to lessen their workload or highlighting the potential positive outcomes of your actions. Be mindful of the impression you make on others; a positive interpersonal style enhances your ability to build productive relationships, whereas a negative style can be detrimental.

Seeking feedback from trusted colleagues on how you are perceived can provide valuable insights into improving your interactions. Promote a spirit of cooperation rather than competition by being open about your thought processes and inviting others to share theirs. Before pushing for a specific solution, generate and consider a range of possibilities, allowing room for adjustments by others. This approach helps maintain focus on shared goals and invites open dialogue about potential challenges and solutions. Address disagreements constructively by asking clarifying questions and understanding the rationale behind differing viewpoints. When conflicts arise, manage them directly but politely and in private, focusing on the issue rather than personal attributes. <u>When faced with a differing viewpoint, don't jump to defend your own</u>. Instead, ask clarifying questions. What specific concerns does the other person have? What reasoning underlies their perspective? And finally, you may shift the conversation from "who's right" to "how can we move forward" and work together to brainstorm solutions that address everyone's concerns. By allowing room for others to articulate their positions and potentially concede on minor points, you help maintain team harmony and move towards resolving issues collectively. This balanced and respectful approach not only fosters better relationships but also ensures that you are an integral and productive member of any team.

Empowering Others to Achieve Collective Goals

Delegation is a critical skill for leaders, offering dual benefits: it not only frees up your time but also fosters motivation and development within your team. <u>Leaders likes to free themselves from getting bogged down in the details to allow themselves to focus on strategic thinking, big-picture goals, and other high-level tasks that require their unique experience and leadership</u>, and when leaders delegate effectively, they entrust their team members with ownership and responsibility. Learning to delegate effectively can be challenging but is essential for both personal leadership growth and team empowerment.

To delegate effectively, start by building trust and taking the time to develop your team members' skills. It's important to remember that delegation does not mean relinquishing responsibility. Instead, it requires a structured approach to ensure clear understanding of expectations. Assign tasks based on individual skills or developmental needs, ideally giving team members responsibilities that stretch their current capabilities slightly. This approach encourages growth and increases engagement. Good delegation involves matching the complexity of the task with the delegate's capacity, enhancing their chance for success. Once a task is delegated, monitor progress through established, time-bound checkpoints or outcome-based milestones, which helps maintain oversight without the need for micromanagement. Encourage open communication, letting team members know they can seek guidance when needed, but refrain from intrusive behaviors. Intervene only if outcomes are not meeting expectations. By following these steps, you can effectively use delegation to enhance individual and group performance, leading to more efficient achievement of organizational goals.

Openness and Innovation

To effectively tap into the collective intelligence of your team, initiate brainstorming sessions that are structured around best practices.

<u>Brainstorming brings together different perspectives and experiences, leading to a wider range of ideas than any individual could come up with alone</u>. This approach ensures that all ideas are considered, allowing every team member the opportunity to contribute. Such sessions are often enriched by unexpected insights that can surface from diverse sources. To maximize creativity, create a protected environment that shields the group from external interruptions and pressures, particularly those demanding premature outcomes. Incorporate stakeholder feedback early in the project process to align the deliverables and outcomes with broader organizational goals, while remaining flexible in the methods used to achieve these targets. This integration allows the project scope to evolve based on direct input from those it will impact.

Encourage your team to seek inspiration beyond the organization by exploring external examples of innovation and best practices. Collaborating with professional peers outside of your business line can also provide fresh perspectives on overcoming current challenges and may offer adaptable solutions. Furthermore, solicit feedback from these peers on your business proposals, presentations, or project plans. External perspectives can be invaluable in refining your strategies and clarifying the key messages you intend to communicate, ensuring they resonate well with the intended audience.

Effective Team Interactions and Contributions

Understanding the stages of team development—Forming, Storming, Norming, and Performing—is essential for facilitating effective team interactions. Recognize the behaviors associated with each stage and assist the team in transitioning smoothly to the next phase through targeted team-building activities. Champion high performance by setting meaningful challenges, appreciating team members' efforts, providing autonomy and necessary resources, and taking an active interest in their tasks. Establish clear, measurable outcomes and celebrate successes both during and at the completion of projects. To truly understand and motivate your team, identify each member's unique skills and motivators.

Conduct monthly one-on-one meetings to explore their motivations and career goals, which helps tailor support and development opportunities effectively. <u>Invest in team development by organizing visits to customers, suppliers, and other organizational units, and provide personalized coaching and feedback</u>. Emphasize diversity in team composition to include a range of backgrounds, skills, and perspectives, ensuring a blend of roles such as coordinators, idea generators, completers, researchers, and networkers.

Ensure that the team balances its focus equally between the task at hand and relationship building. Set clear objectives and individual goals and hold regular meetings to monitor progress and adherence to deadlines. Celebrate performance milestones and, if performance issues arise, consider engaging a team coach. An external coach, whether from HR or an outside expert, can offer objective insights and help identify and resolve behaviors impacting team performance. This approach not only enhances team efficiency but also builds a resilient, collaborative, and highly effective team environment.

Unity and Collaboration Across the Organization

To discourage the divisive 'we vs. they' mindset within teams, it's important to challenge negative perceptions and encourage a broader understanding of every stakeholder's role and value. Start by ensuring that your team not only recognizes but also respects the contributions of all organizational stakeholders. One effective strategy is to arrange field trips or assignments that expose team members to different parts of the organization, broadening their perspectives and fostering a sense of unity. Align team behaviors with the organization's core values and provide tailored coaching and feedback to address any discrepancies. Integrating a member from an external organization into your team for specific projects can also be a transformative experience, promoting cross-team understanding and collaboration.

<u>Additionally, clearly explain to your team how they fit into the overall value chain</u>, detailing both their contributions and those of other teams.

This approach helps team members see the bigger picture and appreciate their role as part of a larger team, thus reducing 'us vs. them' thinking and enhancing organizational synergy.

Facilitating Smooth Execution Without Limits

Effectively removing barriers in any project or team setting requires a strategic and proactive approach. Begin by identifying potential risks and developing mitigation strategies. If issues arise that threaten project success, escalate them promptly to your supervisor to garner necessary support and resources. Crafting a strong business case is essential for effectively negotiating the resources your project needs. Maintain and cultivate give-and-take relationships with key individuals throughout the organization—upward, downward, and laterally. Regular communication is crucial to keep these relationships strong and beneficial. Enforce team rules that discourage members from undermining collective decisions and commitments, addressing any negative behavior immediately to maintain team unity and focus. <u>Anticipate and plan for resistance to change by incorporating a comprehensive stakeholder engagement plan in every new project or initiative</u>. This should include assessing whether those affected by the project possess the necessary skills to adapt to new processes and policies. If gaps exist, prioritize training and development within your project plan to ensure smooth transitions and adoption. This holistic approach not only mitigates risks but also enhances project viability and success through improved stakeholder collaboration and readiness.

At the end, teamwork is essential in achieving organizational goals as it combines diverse skills, experiences, and perspectives to solve complex problems more effectively. It creates a collaborative environment where ideas can grow, and innovation thrives. Through teamwork, individuals learn from each other and enhance their skills, while building relationships that contribute to a more cohesive work culture. Moreover, teamwork facilitates the efficient allocation of resources, ensuring that projects are completed successfully and on schedule. Recognizing the value of teamwork is fundamental to a productive, engaging, and resilient workplace.

TRUST

Credibility and trust are fundamental to the success of any team and company. For leaders aiming to excel, their actions should always and consistently align with their words and promises. As a leader, you set the tone and serve as a role model for trustworthiness and credibility. Your behavior establishes the standards that will be emulated throughout the organization. When you demonstrate integrity in your actions, you not only enhance your own leadership effectiveness but also inspire all employees to uphold these values, fostering a culture of trust and respect across the entire company.

Ensuring Fairness and Consistency

As a leader, you should regularly assess your interactions with team members to ensure you are treating everyone fairly and consistently. This involves self-monitoring to identify any biases or patterns, such as showing less respect to lower performers, individuals with lesser status, or those from different cultural or organizational backgrounds. Take proactive measures to rectify any inequities in your behavior. Ensure that all stakeholders have equal access to necessary information, avoiding the use of information as a selective reward or relationship-building tool. Maintain uniform standards of behavior, ensuring that actions acceptable for high performers are also acceptable for others. Be vigilant about not applying different standards based on gender, age, nationality, ethnic origin, or religion. Soliciting feedback from diverse group members can provide valuable insights into how your actions are perceived. During meetings, make a conscious effort to include everyone, giving equal opportunity for participation. Take time after meetings or one-on-ones to consider your interactions. <u>Did everyone get a chance to speak? Did you give equal weight to different ideas?</u> Encourage quieter or more reserved individuals to express their opinions, thereby developing an inclusive environment where all voices are heard and valued.

Consistency in Practice and Policy

Adhering to your company's Code of Ethics is vital when handling sensitive information, especially in areas that demand strict confidentiality and integrity. These documents are not only a resource but a guide to ethical behavior within the organization. If you encounter ambiguities or uncertainties in complying with these policies, consult with your legal team to ensure your actions align with both the spirit and the letter of the law. Actively participate in the policy feedback loop by reporting any discrepancies or inefficiencies you observe in current policies, facilitating their improvement and ensuring they are applied equitably across the board. <u>When making exceptions to standard rules, maintain transparent reasoning to ensure that these exceptions are based on objective facts rather than personal relationships</u>. Additionally, when evaluating performance, apply consistent standards across all demographics, including gender, age, nationality, ethnic origin, or religion, to uphold fairness and prevent bias. This commitment to ethical consistency not only reinforces personal integrity but also strengthens the overall ethical framework of the organization.

Reliability in Professional Commitments

Maintaining reliability and trustworthiness in a professional setting means not over-promising or exaggerating your capacity to deliver. While it might seem helpful now, making commitments that you cannot fulfill can damage your credibility and be perceived as a failure to follow through. Reflect on past instances where you may have fallen short in this area and consider adopting alternative approaches in the future to avoid repetition of these errors.

Act cautiously and avoid rushing to conclusions. Take the necessary time to make well-considered decisions, ensuring your actions consistently align with your commitments. Diligently attend meetings and appointments as agreed and utilize effective time management systems to keep your commitments on track. Openly communicate with your co-workers about the behaviors you are trying to improve and seek their assistance and feedback.

This not only helps in making a concerted effort towards change but also keeps you accountable and focused on your personal goals. Such practices support a culture of reliability and respect, enhancing both personal and organizational success.

Responsibility for Actions

Accepting responsibility for one's own performance and actions is a key trait of a responsible and respected professional. <u>It is required to admit to mistakes promptly and communicate transparently with everyone affected, detailing potential impacts and taking ownership of the error—whether it occurred individually or within your team.</u> Public acknowledgment of mistakes, when necessary, reinforces personal accountability and demonstrates humility, enhancing your credibility and trustworthiness.

Use clear, unambiguous language to communicate, avoiding statements that could be misconstrued as promises, to minimize confusion. Shifting blame to others or external circumstances undermines accountability. Remember, you cannot rightly claim credit for successes if you are not willing to accept responsibility for failures. Pay attention to the language you use when discussing project setbacks; focus on presenting facts and solutions rather than excuses. This approach not only helps in rectifying the situation but also builds your reputation as a solution-oriented and reliable leader.

Personal Bias in Decision-Making

To ensure decisions are based on facts rather than personal biases, agendas, or stereotypes, it is essential to gather information from multiple sources. Resist the inclination to seek only data that supports your preconceived notions. Demonstrating a team-oriented approach by using inclusive language like 'we' and 'the team' helps distribute recognition fairly and avoids self-centered narratives. Be introspective about your motives; acknowledging personal desires or benefits openly can prevent perceptions of deceit, especially when decisions might favor you or your organization.

It is also vital to consult with individuals from diverse backgrounds before finalizing important decisions. This practice helps achieve a balanced interpretation of the data, enriching your perspective and enhancing the credibility of your conclusions. By embracing these strategies, you not only make more informed and impartial decisions but also foster a culture of transparency and trust within your organization.

Delivering Tough Information with Integrity

When tasked with delivering difficult information, it's decisive to communicate in a clear, straightforward manner. Prepare by formulating two or three concise statements that are fact-based and defensible, minimizing the influence of emotions. If the information is personal, ensure it is delivered privately and at an appropriate time, taking into consideration the sensitivities involved without being swayed by political factors. Approach these situations with boldness, yet maintain a cautious demeanor to respect the recipient's perspective.

Empathize by considering how you would feel if someone withheld important information from you that could have amended a problematic situation. This can guide you to act ethically and transparently. Adhere to your principles and follow established processes diligently. Choose your battles wisely; overemphasizing negative information can lead to others discounting your messages. Maintaining a balance in your approach will help preserve your credibility and ensure that your communications are taken seriously and respectfully.

Aligning Actions with Values

Maintaining consistency in your values and principles is critical for building trust within your organization. Be conscious of any internal conflicts and avoid sending mixed messages, which can confuse and erode trust among your team members. Ensure that your messages remain consistent across different audiences, adjusting only the tone and wording to suit specific groups while keeping the underlying ideas unchanged.

Actions should always match words; demonstrate genuine concern for others through your availability, approachability, and readiness to assist. By embodying the values you espouse, you reinforce your commitment to ethical standards and foster an environment where integrity is both expected and respected.

Standing Firm on Principles

To effectively convey a clear sense of one's core leadership values, it is essential to consistently communicate these values and defend them unwaveringly. <u>Avoid succumbing to external pressures that tempt you to deviate from what you believe is right.</u> Having a clear understanding of your core principles as a leader makes it easier to identify when external pressure is pushing you in the wrong direction. Reflect on what's most important to you - fairness, transparency, integrity? Provide full and honest responses to difficult questions, as withholding information can be perceived as dishonesty or a lack of courage and integrity. Be mindful of the comments you make about others; negative remarks, even if agreed upon in the moment, can lead others to question what might be said about them in their absence. Such behavior can undermine the respect and trust you strive to build within your team. <u>In extreme situations, you may need to walk away from a situation that compromises your values. This can be difficult, but remember, a strong leader stands by their convictions.</u>

Broadcast Trust to Everyone

Instilling confidence in others about your trustworthiness involves respecting confidences and clearly communicating the boundaries of this confidentiality, especially when ethical issues are involved. Freely share information rather than withholding it, as transparency fosters collaboration and increases organizational efficiency. If there are doubts about your trustworthiness, take the time to understand the reasons behind these perceptions and examine any behaviors that may contribute to this view. Addressing these concerns head-on not only clarifies misunderstandings but also strengthens your credibility and the trust others place in you.

This approach is fundamental to fostering a culture of trust and integrity within the organization.

At the end, "trust" is critically important in any company. It serves as the foundation for building strong relationships among team members, between employees and management, and with external stakeholders such as customers and partners. Trust enhances communication, facilitates collaboration, and elevate a big and positive workplace culture, which are all essential for achieving high performance and sustained success. When trust is present, teams are more likely to embrace change, take calculated risks, and innovate. Conversely, a lack of trust can lead to inefficiencies, conflict, and a decrease in employee morale and retention. Overall, trust is a key ingredient in creating a resilient and thriving organization.

Part IV: Advanced Leadership Skills

Leadership is not about being in charge. It is about taking care of those in your charge.

Simon Sinek

SUPPORT AND INFLUENCE

Effective leadership is significantly enhanced by the ability to obtain active support for organizational strategies, projects, and goals across diverse stakeholder groups. When stakeholders feel heard, valued, and involved, they're more likely to champion the organization's goals. This translates to smoother implementation, and a stronger sense of ownership. This skill becomes increasingly significant as leaders ascend the organizational ladder, where they encounter a broader array of stakeholders, including both internal and external parties beyond their direct control. <u>The capacity to influence is integral to a leader's success.</u> It involves a nuanced understanding of various stakeholders' needs, allowing leaders to encourage genuine commitment rather than mere compliance. Effective influencers adapt their leadership styles to fit the situation, demonstrating flexibility, observance, and persuasion. By mastering these elements, leaders can effectively sway the decisions and actions of peers, superiors, customers, vendors, and other key players, directly linking their ability to influence with their overall success in achieving results.

Show your Convictions in a Sound Rational and Emotional Manner

When conveying personal conviction and enthusiasm for your ideas, you must communicate in a manner that resonates both emotionally and factually with your audience. Preparing to present an innovative product or service to senior management involves not just outlining the benefits but also connecting on an emotional level. Practice your presentation in front of various audiences—be it your manager, colleagues, or family members—to refine your delivery and ensure clarity. Focus on articulating the benefits tailored to each audience, emphasizing what's in it for them to foster engagement and support.

For a logical and influential argument requires thorough preparation. Before any meeting, it's imperative to define your objectives and the key points you want to communicate. Consider what you want your audience to remember after the meeting and consider the time constraints and the background knowledge of your audience. By doing so, you can tailor your message effectively, ensuring that it resonates with your audience and achieves your desired impact. Anticipate potential questions and plan your responses to maintain a smooth flow during your presentation. Adopting the principle of 'less is more,' clearly state your main message in a single sentence and then methodically support it with concise, compelling information. This strategic approach ensures your arguments are not only persuasive but also memorable, enhancing your influence and effectiveness as a communicator.

Aligning Ideas with Business Objectives

Presenting your ideas requires clearly illustrating how they align with your organization's specific business needs and the benefits they offer. Start by articulating the "so what" of your proposal—this means emphasizing the tangible outcomes and bottom-line benefits that your idea or recommendation will bring. To ensure these benefits are recognized and valued, establish measurable indicators that can track the impact and progress of your solution over time.

Understanding the business priorities of your audience is essential to tailor your message effectively. What might be critical for one department could be irrelevant for another, so it's important to adapt your argument to resonate with the specific concerns and goals of the audience you're addressing. If you are uncertain about these priorities, take proactive steps to ask directly or spend time within the relevant department to gain a deeper insight into their operations and challenges. This approach not only strengthens the relevance of your proposal but also demonstrates your commitment to holistic organizational improvement.

Overcoming Objections

To effectively connect your ideas with the concerns, interests, and perspectives of others, mastering the art of active listening is vital. This involves restating and recapping what others have expressed to ensure you have grasped the essence of their positions accurately. Consider your audience's needs and how they are likely to react to your message, and tailor your communication to appeal to their interests while minimizing potential negative reactions. Adapt your tone, pace, style, and the method of communication to both the audience and the content of your message, ensuring it resonates effectively and appropriately.

When encountering resistance or objections, actively seek feedback from those who opposed your ideas or proposals to understand their perspectives better and learn what could have been done differently. <u>Before diving into why someone disagrees, ensure you fully understand their perspective</u>. Ask clarifying questions and actively listen to their concerns. Remember, disagreement doesn't have to be a roadblock. Anticipate potential areas of resistance by engaging with stakeholders early, integrating their feedback into your planning process, and understanding their priorities. Sometimes, simply negotiating timelines for delivery can help address and overcome objections, allowing for a smoother implementation of your initiatives. This approach not only helps refine your strategies but also builds stronger, more collaborative relationships with anyone.

Gaining Support

To effectively gain support and commitment for new ideas or action plans, it's important to first identify the stakeholders whose support is essential. Assess each person's stance regarding your proposal—whether they are for, against, or neutral—and develop tailored strategies to address each position. Engage in brainstorming to explore various tactics that could influence the situation positively, focusing on those most likely to succeed. Additionally, enhancing your negotiation skills is crucial; seek insights from colleagues known for their win-win negotiation approaches and apply these strategies to your scenarios.

When building support among key decision-makers, recognize that influence may not always align with seniority. It's important to consider both the formal structure and the informal networks within your organization. Engage key stakeholders informally and one-on-one before any significant formal meetings. This preliminary interaction allows you to articulate your ideas clearly, address potential concerns, and identify areas of common interest. Establishing this groundwork is often vital for fostering agreement and ensuring successful, mutually beneficial outcomes in formal decision-making processes.

Influencing Agendas and Opinions

To proactively shape stakeholder agendas and opinions, it's essential to base your arguments on solid data and an objective evaluation of your department or function. This strategic approach helps in setting and influencing the future direction of the organization. Clearly articulate your vision and position in a concise manner, preparing an 'elevator speech' that effectively communicates your perspective to key stakeholders. Additionally, leverage external insights by connecting with vendors and consultants who have experience with similar organizations. Their external viewpoints can provide valuable informal advice on strategic advancements and help you shape informed opinions among stakeholders.

Balancing Persistence with Relationships

Driving business results demands resilience; don't let criticism deter your leadership. While it's important to consider feedback and adjust your approach as necessary, also recognize situations where opinions are divided, and resilience becomes necessary. <u>It is no secret that leaders are constantly under scrutiny, and some criticism will be inevitable. It's important to not let every comment derail you.</u> There will be times when you'll need to push forward with a vision despite some dissent. This requires confidence in your decisions and a clear understanding of the goals.

In efforts to secure stakeholder support, maintain a firm commitment to your goals but remain flexible about the methods to achieve them. Encourage open dialogue, allowing stakeholders to express concerns and emotions. This openness supports an environment where mutual understanding can flourish, paving the way for collaborative, win-win outcomes. Patience and a willingness to find common ground are key in maintaining positive relationships while achieving business objectives.

At the end, good leaders can profoundly influence a company by setting a clear vision and inspiring employees to strive towards common goals. They foster a culture of transparency, integrity, and accountability, which cultivates trust and boosts morale. Effective leaders actively listen to and value the input of their teams, encouraging innovation and adaptability in response to industry changes. They motivate employees by recognizing achievements and providing opportunities for professional growth. Moreover, by making strategic decisions based on a deep understanding of the business landscape, leaders drive organizational success and resilience. Through their behavior and choices, good leaders not only shape the immediate work environment but also impact the long-term trajectory of the company, ensuring it remains competitive and responsive to customer needs.

WORKING FOR THE RESULTS

To excel as leaders, individuals must adeptly manage multiple priorities while striking a proper balance among standards, costs, and operational efficiency. Demonstrating proficiency in this realm requires mastering the art of concentrating on critical deliverables and strategically distributing tasks among team members in a manner that supports both professional growth and motivation. <u>Leaders must also effectively communicate a sense of urgency and enthusiasm, to achieve results</u>. However, unrealistic deadlines can be de-motivating, but clear and achievable deadlines isn't. By setting achievable deadlines, leaders propel the organization towards ambitious goals delivering substantial business and financial outcomes.

Thrives Independently

Prioritize measuring tangible results rather than simply accounting for hours worked or the volume of tasks completed. Distinguish between what is important and what is urgent, dedicating weekly time to address significant issues. Implement the "Calendar Test" by monitoring how you spend your time over a week, then analyze this data to assess if your time allocation aligns with your goals, values, and priorities.

Each day before leaving work, plan the tasks you need to tackle the following day. Undertake a time management course to sharpen your organizational abilities if you haven't yet. Clearly define your priorities and then categorizing tasks into four quadrants: High Value and Urgent, High Value and Not Urgent, Low Value but Urgent, and Low Value and Not Urgent. Reevaluate the necessity of tasks in the last category. Regularly discuss with your superior to ensure your priorities are synchronized with their expectations, especially important if either of you is new to your roles, as this may require more frequent alignment meetings compared to a well-established working relationship.

Execute Necessary Tasks

Start by defining what "necessary" means in this context. Are these tasks essential for daily operations, project deadlines, or legal requirements? Once you have a clear definition, you can identify the tasks that fall under this category. Create a matrix with "Urgency" on one axis and "Importance" on the other. Necessary tasks will likely be high urgency (need to be done now) and high importance (critical to achieving goals).

Set personal and team objectives, embracing stretch goals that encourage involvement in their creation; this often enhances productivity as individuals work clearer targets. Establish milestones to monitor progress and provide frequent feedback to keep everyone on track. If you're uncertain about the most effective methods to achieve your goals, delve into researching best practices, including project management principles, total quality management, or Six Sigma, to determine which approach aligns best with your circumstances and team dynamics. Engage with process improvement specialists within your organization and organize events to optimize your workflows. Recognize if your strength lies in executing tasks independently while facing challenges in achieving results through others. Identify tasks suitable for delegation and take proactive steps to empower your team members, enabling them to take ownership and effectively deliver on their responsibilities.

A 'Yes We Can' Attitude and Optimistic Outlook

Instill a sense of optimism and ownership within your team by framing challenges as opportunities to innovate and approach problems differently. If resources are scarce, adopt a creative mindset to identify potential sources of support. This could involve borrowing resources or negotiating with colleagues to provide developmental opportunities. Encourage your team members to adopt this inventive approach as well. Enhance your ability to influence beyond your immediate work area by focusing on building relationships and finding common ground, rather than merely requesting assistance.

Practice reciprocity, offering something valuable in return for the help you seek. Sometimes, demonstrating commitment and achieving results requires taking bold risks and championing innovative solutions with your team. Avoid the mindset of "it won't work here" and instead concentrate on how to make ideas successful in your environment. Seek insights from experienced individuals in different parts of the organization or industry to explore what might be feasible under your specific conditions. Actively challenge negative attitudes within your team, as a single pessimistic member can impact the collective morale. Leverage humor and strong relationships both within and outside the team to navigate challenges. Push for a proactive culture by encouraging team members to not only identify problems but also propose three potential solutions, specifying their recommended option. This empowers them and reinforces your confidence in their ability to independently resolve issues, further embedding a sense of ownership and commitment throughout your team.

Demonstrates Sustained Effort to Achieve Results

If you find that your job is depleting your energy and enthusiasm, consider consulting with a trusted coach or mentor to reflect on your circumstances. A fresh perspective or supportive guidance can often reignite your motivation and possibly suggest a beneficial change in your professional role or environment. It's crucial to maintain a healthy work-life balance and look after your physical well-being to ensure you are equipped to handle the demands of leadership.

For those who tend to lose momentum on challenging or monotonous tasks, break the work into manageable segments and establish mini milestones. This strategy allows for more frequent progress checks and helps maintain focus. Start tasks well in advance of deadlines to avoid time pressure and ensure steady progress. While persistence is a valuable trait, it's important to recognize when a particular approach isn't yielding results. In such instances, be open to seeking feedback and ready to adjust your strategies if necessary.

This balance between determination and flexibility is key to effective problem-solving and achieving desired outcomes.

High Standards for Self and Others

Ensure that the goals you establish for yourself and your team include significant challenges and opportunities for growth. People are most motivated when they believe their work is meaningful and contributes directly to the organization's success, prompting them to exert extra effort. Involve your team in setting their own milestones and hold them accountable for meeting these deadlines; deviations should be rare rather than commonplace. When targets are missed, engage in constructive dialogue with the responsible individual to explore the repercussions and viable solutions, ensuring they understand their role in rectifying the situation. Regularly assess the distribution and volume of work among your team members, adjusting workflows and tasks as needed to optimize efficiency and effectiveness.

Continuously monitor and evaluate the quality of work your team produces, providing specific and actionable feedback to maintain high standards. Acceptance of mediocre performance sets a precedent, so it's crucial to only tolerate high-quality outputs. Compare your team's work quality against that of external consultants and vendors to establish benchmarks. Identify a role model or exemplary standard in your field and challenge your team to achieve or exceed these levels of excellence.

Accommodates Needs and Interests

Engage with colleagues from other departments to gather insights on how your department's structure might be enhanced to foster better collaboration. Work closely with other divisions affected by your team's decisions and outputs. If coordination issues are persistent, employ process mapping to pinpoint and address inefficiencies in workflows. Utilize project management tools to monitor the progress of cross-departmental projects, ensuring transparency and shared responsibility for outcomes. Include all the stakeholders who are impacted by your projects in the planning and design stages to ensure their needs and expectations are considered from the outset. Regularly solicit feedback from stakeholders through both qualitative and quantitative methods to gauge satisfaction and identify areas needing improvement. Organize focus group meetings with key stakeholders to uncover critical enhancement opportunities. During these sessions, encourage frank discussions and maintain an open and responsive attitude to the feedback provided. This approach not only helps in meeting the varied interests of stakeholders but also enhances mutual understanding and cooperation across the organization.

Rewarding Efforts

Rewarding efforts effectively is essential for any team leader aiming to sustain motivation and drive within the team. Have you ever noticed how a simple acknowledgment can uplift someone's spirits? One powerful strategy is to establish a structured recognition program. This program should celebrate both individual and team achievements, ensuring that positive results are consistently recognized. Imagine the boost in morale when everyone feels valued for their contributions! This can include formal awards, public recognition during meetings, and personalized thank-you notes, which show appreciation for specific contributions.

It's important to tailor rewards to match the preferences and needs of team members, such as offering flexible work hours, professional development opportunities, or small bonuses. <u>The closer the reward is to the effort, the stronger the connection.</u> Acknowledge and reward exceptional work as soon as possible. Regularly soliciting feedback from the team on what types of rewards they find most motivating can also enhance the effectiveness of these efforts. Celebrating good results -milestones or successes- whether big or small, fills the air with positive and supportive work environment. Additionally, recognizing efforts consistently rather than sporadically helps to reinforce a culture of appreciation and continuous improvement. By understanding and valuing the unique contributions of each team member, a leader can build a motivated, loyal, and high-performing team.

Removes Barriers to Achieve Results

Be proactive in your approach by anticipating potential risks and developing strategies to mitigate them before they can adversely affect your goals. Invite individuals from outside your team to evaluate your assumptions about key challenges, utilizing their impartial perspectives to identify any misjudgments.

Advocate for a culture within your organization that encourages the early identification of issues, promoting creative problem-solving among your team members to keep projects on track. Employ data tracking and set milestones to establish an effective early warning system that helps in timely detection and removal of impediments. Implement scenario planning to anticipate various possible future situations. Prepare multiple strategies to address these scenarios, equipping your team to handle potential obstacles efficiently. Don't hesitate to seek assistance when needed; reach out to colleagues and specialized departments for support during unforeseen challenges. Reciprocate by offering help to others, cultivating a cooperative and supportive work atmosphere.

Addresses and Resolves Issues

Act swiftly to identify and rectify organizational shortcomings and failures. When issues are specifically related to the actions of an individual or team, address these problems respectfully and factually to facilitate effective correction. Steer clear of quick fixes that merely treat symptoms rather than tackling the root causes of problems. Always factor in ethical considerations when resolving issues, recognizing that compromising on safety or core values can cause long-term reputational damage to the organization. Ensure accurate diagnosis of problems; if an issue stems from a team member, collaborate with them to uncover underlying causes—whether they be communication gaps, misaligned objectives, insufficient skills, or lack of motivation—before devising an appropriate solution. Whenever possible, keep people informed about issues and actively involve them in the process of designing and implementing solutions.

This inclusive approach not only enhances the effectiveness of the resolution but also builds a collaborative and transparent workplace culture.

At the end, working for the results is a fundamental aspect of effective team leadership. A team leader can achieve this by setting clear, measurable goals that align with the organization's objectives. It's crucial to communicate these goals to the team, ensuring everyone understands their role and the collective targets. Regular progress reviews and feedback sessions help keep the team on track and address any obstacles promptly. Additionally, pushing for a results-oriented culture involves recognizing and rewarding achievements, which motivates team members to maintain high performance. Leveraging data and analytics can provide insights into performance trends and areas for improvement. Effective delegation and resource management ensure that team members are working efficiently towards their objectives. Finally, a leader should lead by example, demonstrating commitment to achieving results, which inspires the team to follow suit. This comprehensive approach not only drives success but also enhances team cohesion and morale, creating a productive and motivated work environment.

EXECUTION

The critical difference between leaders and individual contributors lies in a leader's ability to achieve work through others. Effective leaders create a visible link between organizational strategy and individual goals and priorities. To successfully demonstrate this ability, leaders must monitor both the impact of delegated assignments in driving the organization forward and the skill and efficiency with which their teams execute those goals. By setting clear timelines and milestones and using Key Performance Indicators (KPIs), leaders can anticipate problems and call on additional resources to ensure that projects are delivered on time, within budget, and achieve the necessary outcomes. Effective leaders are distinguished by their ability to balance short and long-term organizational priorities while simultaneously building highly skilled and engaged teams. This balance ensures that immediate objectives are met without compromising future goals, while keeping the door open for improvement and sustained success.

Setting and Communicating Clear Priorities

Before assigning projects, work, and tasks, it's vital to set clear goals that help individuals focus their time and efforts, and understand the relevance of their work. Embracing the concept of Managing by Objectives (MBO) is key. By clearly demonstrating how your goals align with your company's overall strategy, you provide a roadmap that not only clarifies each person's role but also instills a sense of purpose and direction. This alignment is crucial in driving the entire team toward success and achieving remarkable outcomes. Engaging your team in the goal-setting process translates key priorities into individual objectives and targets, knowing that people are most motivated when they have input into how goals are set and measured. It is important to define how goals will be measured and what the rewards and consequences will be for those who exceed, meet, or miss their goals, communicating these expectations both verbally and in writing.

Asking team members to define the scope and resource needs for each of their deliverables allows for better planning. Arranging a team meeting to address any resourcing conflicts and agree on priorities that align with your own helps maintain clarity. Regular team meetings to review the achievement of critical milestones and address project risks are necessary to keep everyone focused and on track.

Provides an Appropriate Level of Guidance and Instruction

Ensure that your company allows you time to address people issues is key, as delegation, coaching, and people management are high value-added activities that should be prioritized in your work schedule. To delegate effectively, communicate clearly, set time frames and goals, and then allow those to whom you have delegated to take control of the task or project. One common problem in delegation is unclear communication upfront. To mitigate this, ask the team or individual to write down their understanding of the task for you to review and agree upon. Recognize that people work differently, so it's important to match the goals to each individual's working style. Some may prefer stretch goals, while others respond better when assured they can achieve the goal ahead of time. Involving each person in the process can facilitate better goal matching. The best delegators are clear on what they want to achieve and when they want it, while leaving the individuals or teams some flexibility in determining how to achieve it. This approach maximizes motivation, as people are most driven when they have autonomy over how they accomplish their tasks.

Keep Your Projects on Track

Establishing clear methods and goals is essential to help you and your teams determine whether projects are on track or at risk of derailment. Be explicit about your expectations from the beginning. Communicate the impact of work on others both inside and outside the department, ensuring the group engages with these internal or external stakeholders to identify and address potential issues before they affect the project.

Create an open environment where employees and teams feel comfortable escalating issues promptly and encourage them to seek coaching and support from you and each other. When you make regular team meetings to share challenges and successes, you will spot and rectify any uncalculated mishap. Including risks and mitigations as a standard part of your project planning process is crucial. Ensure that projects are thoroughly scoped to include resource requirements from the outset, incorporating lead times for acquiring necessary personnel and materials into the project plan. Additionally, consult with others in the organization or externally who have experience with similar projects, learning from the issues they encountered and taking proactive measures to mitigate these in your own project plans.

Allocating Time Appropriately to Make Progress

Being adaptable is essential when managing projects, especially when confronted with unfavorable information. <u>It's important to incorporate feedback from the team if they indicate that the project is not on track or at risk of not achieving the desired outcomes.</u> You must know that your team is often closest to the project details. Their observations can flag potential issues before they snowball. Consistency in direction is crucial; frequently asking team members to shift focus can be demotivating. If a change in direction is necessary, ensure you provide a compelling rationale for the adjustment. When taking on a leadership role in a new area, invest time in understanding what your team is already working on before setting new priorities, and where possible, build upon or reinforce existing objectives. Understanding the cost-benefit relationship of your team's projects is vital; sometimes, it may be more beneficial to increase costs to ensure timely delivery rather than fail to meet deadlines. Define project completion with measurable outcomes to help you and your team assess whether the projects have been successfully concluded and include a review stage after completion to identify any necessary follow-up actions. This approach ensures that time is allocated efficiently, progress is made, and pending tasks are completed effectively.

Delegating Tasks All the Way

Delegating tasks "all the way" means giving as much responsibility and authority as possible, focusing on complete tasks rather than fragmented activities, as this is more motivating for individuals. It's important to delegate assignments that help team members develop new skills, while ensuring they receive proper coaching and guidance. Effective delegators match the complexity of tasks with the abilities of their team members, often involving them in deciding the appropriate task size, as people generally prefer challenging tasks over repetitive ones. Ask your team which of your tasks they believe they could assist with or take over, as even a few delegated tasks can allow you to concentrate on more strategic, high-value activities. Consider why you might be hesitant to delegate; if you prefer handling specific tasks yourself, it might indicate a preference for individual contribution over leadership, which requires enabling others to complete work.

If you struggle with perfectionism or unrealistic expectations, work on trusting your team's contributions and accepting that different approaches can be equally effective. When your team is too busy to take on more tasks, help them prioritize their workload, collectively identifying tasks that can be reassigned or eliminated.

Monitor Your Progress Carefully

Establish effective key performance indicators and milestones at the beginning of projects to enable monitoring achievements and outcomes and to make necessary adjustments if things are not going according to plan. Schedule regular review meetings to check progress against critical milestones with the team. Solicit feedback from your team to ensure they do not feel micromanaged and ask for suggestions on how you can better support project outcomes. Be prepared to step in and support a project when agreed-upon criteria are not being met or expectations are falling short. Engage with the person or team to understand their perspective on the problem and ask how you can assist in getting the project back on track.

When goals or priorities change, meet with affected teams and stakeholders to determine the impact on existing projects and request revised project plans for your review and approval. Hold regular team meetings to ensure everyone is aware of the group's projects and priorities, identifying interdependencies and preventing duplication. If necessary, encourage teams to refocus their priorities to ensure that the organization delivers on critical strategic priorities.

Regular Follow-ups for Goals

Establish a process to monitor progress against goals, as people appreciate gauging their progress and seeing how they are performing against project milestones. Provide as much feedback as possible, as soon as possible, since most people are motivated by feedback—it helps them adjust their actions and demonstrates that their efforts are valued. Avoid saving constructive feedback for year-end reviews when it is too late for adjustments. Follow through with both positive and negative rewards and consequences. Celebrate with those who exceed expectations, commend those who went the extra mile to meet goals, and analyze what went wrong with those who missed their targets. Ensuring that you deliver the promised rewards maintains a high level of trust in your leadership.

Securing Resources When Needed

Ensure that you establish effective priorities, distinguishing between mission-critical projects, important tasks, and those that are nice to do if time allows. This distinction will help you refocus resources when mission-critical or important projects require additional support. Challenge teams or employees who request extra support by asking how they can help themselves. Encourage them to work on project elements in parallel rather than sequentially to stay on track and to focus on mission-critical aspects rather than getting bogged down in less important details. Ask the team or individual to suggest additional resources they could leverage, ensuring they propose a recommended solution rather than just presenting a problem.

Be cautious not to disempower them or take back project ownership. Review your area's project and resource plans to see if employees can be temporarily reassigned to provide additional support without compromising other departmental work. Hold a team meeting to foster a collaborative environment where the team can work together to resolve issues. Redefine goals and accountabilities as necessary; some work might be further delegated or simplified. Reach out to peers in other organizations for support and be prepared to reciprocate when they need assistance. Additionally, consider whether some tasks can be sub-contracted or outsourced to alleviate the workload.

Plan Meetings to Ensure Objectives Are Met

Meetings can often be time-consuming and unproductive, so it's important to ensure that a meeting is the right forum for the topic at hand. Consider whether a conference call or email might be more effective. Adequate preparation is key; if you're seeking agreement or decisions, gauge the opinions of critical stakeholders beforehand and incorporate their views into your proposal to improve the chances of reaching consensus. Clearly identify the purpose of the meeting and inform participants of the agenda in advance, allowing them to prepare and bring relevant information, and to determine if they are the best representatives for their project or group. Establish the desired outcomes from the start, as the meeting's agenda and format will vary depending on whether you seek feedback, provide information, or require consensus and decisions. Ensure you bring all necessary information to achieve the desired outcome by the end of the meeting. Invite the right people, particularly those who have the authority to make decisions if needed. Assign specific roles to participants, such as a timekeeper and someone to note decisions and action items, to maximize productivity. Prioritize agenda items so the group can focus on critical topics first, ensuring that essential outcomes are achieved even if time runs short.

Facilitate discussions by encouraging participation from everyone, asking questions, and listening to contributions.

Summarize periodically to keep the group focused and on track and consider using a flip chart or whiteboard to help develop and organize the group's thoughts. Set ground rules to maximize meeting efficiency, such as asking participants to turn off phones and close laptops. If the meeting extends beyond 90 minutes, schedule breaks to allow participants to address external business issues and return focused. Finally, ensure that meeting outcomes are recorded and that action items are integrated into relevant project plans, distributing copies to all participants.

Balancing Operational Results with the Accomplishment of Key Initiatives

To balance operational results with key initiatives, start by reviewing resource allocation to ensure it aligns with your strategic priorities, including both time and personnel. Identify any constraints that may hinder the execution of your strategy and develop plans to address these issues. Once you have outlined your strategy and priorities, seek feedback from others to identify potential problems. Use this feedback to create a detailed resourcing plan that encompasses processes, structures, staffing, and skills. Encourage your teams to assess their current tasks and identify areas of work that will become less significant as key initiatives are accomplished. Ask them to suggest how to refocus activities and ensure they have the necessary skills to meet new challenges.

Challenge your teams to pinpoint activities that can be discontinued or reassigned to other areas within the organization to eliminate overlap and duplication. Have your team identify goals that contribute to maintaining and improving current operations while also advancing key initiatives to build the future organization. Together, determine the appropriate sequencing and prioritization of these goals to effectively balance short-term results with long-term strategic objectives. Create a roadmap that outlines the order in which goals will be tackled. Short-term wins that contribute to long-term objectives should be prioritized early on. This is a collaborative process. By setting priorities and sequencing goals, you'll increase the chances of success.

Accountability for Achieving Results at All Levels

Begin by being very clear on business goals throughout your organization, asking leaders at each level to discuss these goals with their teams and define their specific contributions toward achieving them. Ensure that strategic goals are integrated into the goals and priorities of everyone in the performance management system. Hold regular meetings with all your leaders to review progress against critical milestones and discuss any necessary corrective actions. Maintain appropriate follow-up and consequence management at all organizational levels—individual, team, and organizational. Reward, recognize, and celebrate successes while also addressing underperformance at the appropriate level through discussion, understanding, and targeted actions.

In the end, the importance of execution for achieving results cannot be overstated. Effective execution transforms strategic plans into tangible outcomes, driving the success and growth of an organization. Without proper execution, even the most innovative ideas and well-thought-out strategies remain mere concepts. Execution ensures that resources are utilized efficiently, processes are optimized, and goals are met within the desired timelines. It involves meticulous planning, clear communication, and consistent monitoring of progress. By focusing on execution, businesses can adapt to changes, overcome challenges, and stay competitive in the market. Ultimately, execution is the bridge between vision and reality, making it a critical factor in the attainment of business objectives.

SAFETY TALK

Safety is the one competency that applies to everyone who works at any company. It is a core value and a mandated goal for all leaders and employees. The top priority for every leader in the organization is to ensure the safety and health of the employees and the communities in which they operate. The key is to ensure that employees are aware of risks and take active steps to look after their own health and safety, as well as the health and safety of their co-workers. Your effectiveness in driving success in this area is critical to the Company's reputation as an employer, a corporate citizen, and a business partner to its customers.

Enforcing Safety

Regularly conduct loss prevention tours and ask your direct reports to do the same, ensuring they report and monitor the implementation of corrective actions. Set and communicate clear goals and standards for work, possibly mapping individual processes on a single page to clearly convey the expected work standards for each team member. Actively involve your team in the planning and implementation process to secure their support. Allocate the necessary tools and resources to implement your safety plan effectively. Consult with productivity departments for expert guidance and assistance in planning and implementing the company's system. Include loss prevention criteria when awarding outside contracts. Ensure all assets within your work area are maintained properly throughout their lifecycle to protect people, property, and the environment.

Awareness For Best Practices

Regularly hold team briefings on safety topics particularly relevant to your work area. Establish loss prevention forums to encourage input and feedback from all levels of the workforce, contractors, and suppliers.

Cultivate a culture of **zero tolerance** regarding health and safety, ensuring appropriate and proportionate consequence management for those who fail to comply with company safety standards. Invite new starters to highlight any issues they perceive as unsafe, as their fresh perspectives can provide valuable insights.

Develop a safety communication calendar to facilitate the timely flow of information within your area, utilizing various communication media such as posters, emails, and e-learning to ensure the message reaches all audiences. Arrange regular training sessions to ensure all team members have the necessary knowledge to work safely. Ensure that contract employees and their sub-contractors are trained in Saudi Aramco safety rules and meet the company's defined competence levels in their craft or skill. This comprehensive approach will enhance safety awareness and adherence to best practices, promoting a safer work environment for everyone involved.

Overseeing Safety Metrics and Processes

Collaborate with your team to identify a dashboard of key health and safety metrics, reviewing them regularly to spot trends. Display these metrics and communicate them during team briefings, highlighting key messages and engaging with team members to identify possible solutions. Benchmark your organization against other internal and similar external organizations, setting targets to improve performance on key metrics. Use both leading indicators, such as the number of management reviews, hazard assessments, and audit actions closed, and lagging indicators, such as injury frequency, number of spills, and the value of property or production losses, to provide a balanced view of your loss prevention performance. Spend time during each PMP review discussing the safety performance of each team member, considering factors such as visible support of loss prevention policy, housekeeping standards, injury and accident data, and compliance within their area of responsibility. This comprehensive approach ensures that safety metrics and processes are effectively monitored, fostering a safer work environment.

Highlighting Safety Violations

Ensure that lessons learned from risk and hazard identification or loss prevention violations are communicated to the team and disseminated to all employees. For serious incidents, hold a more in-depth after-action review with the team involved. Analyze the response, identify areas for improvement, and develop corrective actions. Share information beyond your work unit so that others in similar environments can benefit from your experiences. Escalate information to address any potential process or policy gaps at the corporate level. Remember that the disciplinary process may and should be used in cases of loss prevention violations.

Find Opportunities for Risk Reduction

Encourage hazard identification by setting targets for workforce groups and recognizing the team with the highest score on a quarterly and annual basis. Nominate employees within your workgroup to act as champions for implementing and monitoring corporate loss prevention initiatives at a local level. Integrate loss prevention and ergonomic considerations into the purchase of new capital equipment, building designs, and office layouts. Ensure these considerations are also included in your project planning process, allocating sufficient time and resources to maintain safety. Encourage employees to think of hazards beyond the normal workplace to foster a comprehensive safety mindset. Ensure that new employees and those who have transferred internally are medically fit to work in your area, and conduct baseline medical surveillance for employees exposed to hazardous environments, such as audiometric tests for those working in high-noise areas.

Encourage employees to look out for one another and to identify and report potential hazards in the workplace. Recognize groups and individuals who exhibit strong health and safety behaviors and have them mentor new or less experienced employees. Ensure that all employees are competent to perform their assigned operational and maintenance tasks and possess the required knowledge of your company's safety rules and standards.

Conduct tours of your area and engage employees in discussions about the expected standards of safety behavior, summarizing the results and discussing them with your direct reports to identify areas for improvement.

Taking Action to Enhance or Modify Potential Risks

Demonstrate the courage to shut down processes or modify systems that pose significant risks. Learn from external best practices to understand how similar operations establish robust safety systems and processes. Classify all injuries and near misses by loss consequences to determine the necessary level of investigation, follow-up, and education. Prioritize follow-ups on hazard reporting, focusing on corrective actions that mitigate the highest potential risks. Hold meetings with your team to identify foreseeable emergency scenarios that may affect your area, and develop comprehensive emergency response and recovery plans for high-likelihood, high-impact situations. Communicate these plans effectively to ensure preparedness.

Risk Analysis

Conducting an effective risk analysis involves reviewing major hazards and identifying the need for risk reduction measures. Assess the likelihood of each risk occurring—whether high, medium, or low—and evaluate the potential consequences to define appropriate risk reduction strategies. Significant investments in time, capital, training, and personnel may be necessary for risks with high likelihood and/or high impact. Allocate a portion of your annual budget to update and enhance safety systems. Consider ergonomics when making capital equipment purchasing decisions to ensure safe and efficient operations. Ensure appropriate staffing levels, especially in high-risk environments or those with atypical shift patterns. <u>Minimize lone working whenever possible and implement additional safety measures when it cannot be avoided</u>. Keep emergency response plans up-to-date and ensure they are understood by all team members.

Regularly practice fire drills and other emergency procedures to maintain preparedness and ensure that everyone knows how to respond in case of an emergency.

At the end, the importance of safety and the well-being of people in any company cannot be overstated. A robust safety culture ensures that employees are protected from workplace hazards, reducing the risk of accidents and injuries. Prioritizing safety will definitely ensure a healthy work environment, which boosts morale, productivity, and overall job satisfaction. It also enhances the company's reputation as a responsible and caring employer, which is crucial for attracting and retaining talent. Moreover, a commitment to safety ensures compliance with legal and regulatory standards, minimizing the risk of costly fines and legal issues. Ultimately, ensuring the well-being of employees not only protects them but also strengthens the company's operational effectiveness and long-term success.

Part V: Decisions, Behavior and Improvement

Whenever you see a successful business, someone once made a courageous decision.

Peter Drucker

THE IMPACT OF DECISIONS

SUPERVISOR

At the **supervisory** level, you have a direct and immediate impact on the day-to-day operations and the morale of team members. Supervisors are often the closest to the frontline employees and are responsible for implementing company policies and procedures on the ground. Their decisions regarding task assignments, conflict resolution, and performance feedback can significantly influence team dynamics and productivity. Effective supervisors ensure clear communication, provide adequate support, and ensure a positive work environment, which enhances employee engagement and job satisfaction. When employees understand expectations, goals, and procedures, they're less likely to feel frustrated or make mistakes.

Conversely, the consequences of poor decisions by a supervisor can be substantial and wide-reaching, affecting not only the immediate team but potentially the entire organization.

The Impact of Bad Supervisors

Decline in Employee Morale and Engagement

A **supervisor**'s decision to overlook or dismiss employee concerns can lead to a decline in morale. For instance, if a supervisor consistently ignores requests for necessary tools or resources, employees may feel undervalued and unsupported. This can lead to disengagement, where employees do not put in their best effort, resulting in decreased productivity. For example, if a team member repeatedly asks for updated software to improve their work efficiency and the supervisor dismisses these requests, the employee may become frustrated and less motivated to perform their duties effectively. For example, Micromanagement, imagine a supervisor who constantly monitors every detail of your work, providing unnecessary feedback and stifling your autonomy. These are just a few examples of how bad supervisors can negatively impact employee morale and engagement. When employees feel undervalued, unsupported, and stressed, their happiness and productivity suffer. This ultimately hurts the company as well.

Increased Turnover Rates

Poor decisions regarding employee treatment and recognition can lead to higher turnover rates. If a **supervisor** fails to acknowledge hard work and does not provide opportunities for advancement or professional growth, employees may seek employment elsewhere. For example, <u>if a high-performing employee is continually passed over for promotion in favor of less qualified individuals due to the supervisor's bias or poor judgment, that employee may leave the company, taking their skills and experience with them</u>. This not only disrupts team dynamics but also incurs additional costs for the company in recruiting and training new employees.

Similarly, as mentioned previously, bad supervisors who micromanage, lack communication, or don't offer support can lead to employee dissatisfaction and drive them to leave.

Decreased Productivity and Efficiency

Ineffective task assignments can result in decreased productivity and efficiency. For instance, if a **supervisor** assigns tasks without considering employees' strengths and skills, tasks may be performed poorly or take longer to complete. For example, if a supervisor assigns a complex project to a team member without the necessary expertise while more qualified individuals are available, the project may suffer from delays and subpar outcomes. This mismanagement can cause bottlenecks and slow down overall progress.

Poor Team Dynamics and Increased Conflict

A **supervisor's** inability to manage conflicts or foster a collaborative environment can lead to poor team dynamics. If a supervisor shows favoritism or fails to address interpersonal issues within the team, it can create a toxic work environment. For example, if a supervisor consistently favors one employee over others, giving them the best assignments and more flexibility, resentment can build among team members, leading to conflicts and a lack of cohesion. This can hinder teamwork and reduce overall productivity.

Compromised Safety and Compliance

Neglecting safety protocols can have serious consequences. These consequences can impact everyone involved, from individual workers to entire companies. For instance, if a **supervisor** decides to cut corners to meet deadlines, ignoring safety procedures, it can result in accidents or violations of regulations. For example, if a supervisor instructs employees to bypass certain safety checks to speed up production, it increases the risk of workplace accidents, which can lead to injuries, legal issues, and financial penalties for the company. Furthermore, <u>news of safety violations can spread quickly, damaging a company's reputation and public image.</u> Customers may be hesitant to do business with a company perceived as unsafe, and attracting and retaining talent can become difficult.

Deterioration of Customer Satisfaction

Poor decision-making that affects the quality of work can lead to decreased customer satisfaction. For example, if a **supervisor** fails to address quality control issues, resulting in defective products or late services, customers may become dissatisfied and take their business elsewhere. For instance, if a supervisor overlooks a quality issue in a manufacturing process to save time, and defective products reach customers, it can lead to returns, complaints, and damage to the company's reputation. A pattern of poor decision-making that consistently impacts quality erodes customer trust. Customers may question the company's ability to deliver on its promises and may be hesitant to do business in the future.

In summary, poor decisions by a supervisor can have a ripple effect, leading to lower morale, higher turnover, decreased productivity, poor team dynamics, compromised safety, and reduced customer satisfaction. These consequences underscore the importance of sound decision-making and effective leadership at the supervisory level.

SUPERINTENDENT (TEAM LEADER)

At the **superintendent** level, decisions have a broader scope, impacting multiple teams or departments within the organization. Superintendents are responsible for coordinating efforts across various units, ensuring that resources are allocated efficiently, and that projects are aligned with the company's strategic goals. Their decisions on resource management, process improvements, and interdepartmental collaboration can significantly affect the organization's operational efficiency and effectiveness. Superintendents play a leading role in bridging the gap between frontline operations and higher management, ensuring that organizational goals are met while addressing any challenges that arise at the departmental level. Superintendents must also be adept at change management, guiding their departments through transitions smoothly and maintaining stability during periods of organizational change.

Effective decision-making at the superintendent level can have a profound impact on productivity and operational success, influencing multiple teams or departments.

The Effect of <u>Good</u> Superintendent

Optimized Resource Allocation

Superintendents are responsible for ensuring that resources such as manpower, equipment, and budget are allocated efficiently. They act as the bridge between planning and execution, overseeing the day-to-day operations. By making informed decisions about resource distribution, superintendents can optimize operations and improve productivity. Example: A superintendent in a manufacturing plant assesses the production schedules and identifies that a particular line is consistently under-resourced, causing delays. By reallocating staff and equipment from a less critical line to this bottleneck, the superintendent ensures smoother operations and increases overall throughput. This decision not only prevents delays but also boosts the output without additional costs.

Enhanced Process Improvement

Superintendents play a key role in identifying and implementing process improvements that enhance efficiency and reduce waste. Example: In a logistics company, the superintendent notices that the process for loading trucks is inefficient, leading to delays and increased labor costs. After analyzing the workflow, the superintendent introduces a new system where trucks are preloaded based on delivery routes and times. This change streamlines the loading process, reduces wait times, and lowers labor costs, leading to significant improvements in delivery times and customer satisfaction.

Improved Interdepartmental Collaboration

Effective **superintendents** facilitate better communication and collaboration between different departments, ensuring that everyone is working towards common goals. Example: In a hospital setting, a superintendent identifies that the lack of communication between the emergency department and the inpatient wards is causing delays in patient admissions. By implementing a new protocol for regular interdepartmental meetings and an integrated electronic health records system, the superintendent ensures timely information sharing. This improves patient flow, reduces wait times, and enhances the overall efficiency of the hospital.

Strategic Problem Solving

Superintendents are often tasked with solving complex problems that affect multiple teams or processes. Effective decision-making in this area can lead to substantial operational gains. Example: In a construction company, the superintendent faces repeated delays due to supply chain disruptions. By negotiating with multiple suppliers and creating a buffer stock of critical materials, the superintendent mitigates the risk of future delays. This proactive approach ensures that construction projects stay on schedule, reducing downtime and increasing productivity.

Effective Change Management

Superintendents are responsible for managing changes within their departments. Their ability to effectively guide their teams through transitions can maintain stability and enhance performance. Example: In a tech company, a superintendent leads the transition to a new project management software. By organizing comprehensive training sessions, providing continuous support, and addressing employee concerns promptly, the superintendent ensures a smooth transition. This results in better project tracking, improved team collaboration, and higher productivity.

Data-Driven Decision Making

Effective **superintendents** utilize data to make informed decisions that enhance operational efficiency and productivity. Example: A superintendent in a retail company uses sales data to identify peak shopping times and adjusts staffing levels accordingly. By ensuring that more staff are available during busy periods and fewer during slow times, the superintendent optimizes labor costs while maintaining high customer service levels. This data-driven approach results in better customer satisfaction and improved sales performance.

Risk Management and Safety Enhancements

Superintendents play a vital role in identifying and mitigating risks, ensuring that operations run smoothly and safely. Superintendents function as the on-site guardians of safety and smooth operations. They wear many hats, but risk mitigation and ensuring a safe work environment are some of their most critical responsibilities. Example: In an oil and gas company, the superintendent identifies potential safety hazards due to aging equipment. By prioritizing the replacement of high-risk machinery and enhancing safety protocols, the superintendent reduces the risk of accidents.

This proactive risk management ensures a safer work environment, reduces downtime due to incidents, and maintains steady productivity.

In summary, effective decision-making at the **superintendent** level can drive significant improvements in productivity and operational success by optimizing resource allocation, enhancing processes, fostering interdepartmental collaboration, solving strategic problems, managing changes effectively, utilizing data for informed decisions, and enhancing safety protocols. These decisions create a ripple effect that improves efficiency, reduces costs, and ultimately contributes to the organization's overall success.

MANAGERS

Managers, occupying a higher leadership position, make decisions that shape the strategic direction of the organization. Their decisions on policy formulation, long-term planning, and organizational culture have far-reaching consequences that influence the entire company. Managers must consider market trends, competitive positioning, and internal capabilities when making decisions that will guide the company's growth and sustainability. They are also responsible for ensuring that the company's vision and mission are effectively communicated and embraced throughout all levels of the organization. Strategic decisions made by managers can determine the organization's success in achieving its long-term goals, while poor decisions can lead to strategic misalignment, loss of market position, and decreased organizational performance. Additionally, managers play a key role in fostering a culture of innovation and continuous improvement, encouraging employees to contribute ideas that drive the company forward.

For managers, striking a balance between short-term operational needs and long-term strategic initiatives is key to ensuring their company remains agile and competitive in a fast-evolving business landscape. Think about the impact of this balance on your organization's future. By adeptly managing both aspects, you position your company to adapt swiftly and effectively, securing a sustainable competitive edge.

The Effect of a <u>Good</u> Manager

Prioritizing Immediate Operational Efficiency

Managers must ensure that day-to-day operations run smoothly and efficiently, addressing any immediate issues that arise without losing sight of long-term goals. Example: In a manufacturing company, a manager notices that a critical machine is frequently breaking down, causing production delays. To address this immediate operational need, the manager allocates budget for urgent repairs and initiates a maintenance schedule to prevent future breakdowns. Simultaneously, the manager includes plans for upgrading the entire production line in the long-term strategic roadmap, ensuring sustainable operational efficiency, and reducing long-term costs.

Aligning Short-Term Projects with Long-Term Goals

Managers should ensure that short-term projects contribute to the company's long-term strategic objectives, creating a cohesive approach to growth and development. Example: A manager in a software development company is tasked with delivering a new feature requested by a major client. While this short-term project is critical for maintaining client satisfaction, the manager aligns the development of this feature with the company's long-term goal of improving overall product usability. By incorporating elements of the feature into the broader product development strategy, the manager ensures that the short-term project also supports long-term strategic goals.

Investing in Workforce Development

Balancing immediate workforce needs with long-term talent development is essential for maintaining a skilled and motivated team that can drive future growth. Example: In a healthcare organization, a **manager** addresses the immediate need for more nursing staff due to a sudden increase in patient volume. To meet this short-term need, the manager hires temporary staff. Simultaneously, the manager invests in long-term training programs for existing staff, providing opportunities for professional development and career advancement. This dual approach ensures that the organization can handle current demands while building a stronger, more skilled workforce for the future.

Agile Planning and Flexibility

Managers must be flexible and adaptable, adjusting plans as necessary to respond to both short-term challenges and long-term opportunities.

Example: In a retail company, a manager develops a long-term strategy to expand the company's e-commerce presence. However, during the holiday season, the manager shifts focus to address immediate operational needs, such as increasing inventory and staffing levels to handle the seasonal surge in demand. After the peak season, the manager returns to the e-commerce strategy, incorporating lessons learned from the holiday operations to refine and strengthen the long-term plan.

Resource Allocation and Budget Management

Effective **managers** allocate resources in a way that addresses immediate needs while also investing in initiatives that support long-term growth. Example: In a tech startup, a manager must balance the need to fund ongoing product development with the requirement to invest in marketing to attract new customers. The manager allocates a portion of the budget to enhance the current product based on user feedback (a short-term operational need) while also setting aside funds for a major marketing campaign aimed at expanding market share (a long-term strategic initiative). This balanced approach ensures that the company can continue to innovate and grow its customer base.

Monitoring Market Trends and Customer Needs

Managers must stay attuned to market trends and customer needs, making decisions that address current demands while positioning the company for future success. In today's dynamic business landscape, successful managers need to be forward-thinking. They must act as a bridge between the present and the future, understanding current market trends and customer needs while making decisions that not only address them but also position the company for long-term success. Example: A manager in a consumer electronics company monitors the increasing demand for smart home devices. To meet short-term market demand, the manager accelerates the release of new smart home products. Concurrently, the manager invests in research and development to explore next-generation technologies, ensuring that the company remains at the forefront of innovation in the long term.

Strategic Risk Management

Balancing short-term and long-term needs involves managing risks in a way that protects the company's immediate interests while positioning it for future opportunities. Example: In a financial services firm, a **manager** identifies a potential regulatory change that could impact current operations. The manager allocates resources to ensure compliance with the new regulations (addressing an immediate need) while also exploring ways to leverage the regulatory change to create new financial products or services. This strategic approach mitigates short-term risks while positioning the company to capitalize on long-term opportunities.

In summary, managers must carefully balance short-term operational needs with long-term strategic initiatives to keep the company agile and competitive. By prioritizing immediate efficiency, aligning projects with strategic goals, investing in workforce development, remaining flexible, managing resources wisely, monitoring market trends, and managing risks strategically, managers can ensure that their organizations thrive in both the present and the future.

BEHAVIOR, DRESS CODE AND REPRESENTATION

SUPERVISORS

Supervisors, being the closest to frontline employees, should embody approachability and practicality. They must behave with integrity, showing consistency in their actions and decisions, which builds trust among their team members. Supervisors should dress in a manner appropriate for the operational environment, balancing professionalism with practicality. For example, in a manufacturing setting, where usually a supervisor has a uniform, this might mean wearing safety gear and work-appropriate attire, demonstrating a hands-on approach. When communicating, supervisors should be clear, concise, and supportive, using everyday language that resonates with their team. They should represent the company's values through their actions, showing dedication to safety, quality, and team cohesion.

Supervisors: Manners

Supervisors hold a pivotal role in crafting the work environment and uplifting the morale of frontline employees. Therefore, their manners are essential in fostering a positive and productive workplace.

Respectfulness: Supervisors should treat all team members with respect, recognizing their contributions and valuing their input. This respect fosters mutual trust and encourages open communication.
Empathy: Demonstrating empathy is key to understanding and addressing the concerns and needs of team members. Supervisors who show genuine concern for their employees' well-being can build stronger, more cohesive teams.

Fairness: Supervisors must be fair in their decisions and treatment of employees, avoiding favoritism and ensuring that everyone has equal opportunities for growth and development. This removes the possibility of bias based factors unrelated to qualifications.

Patience: Patience is critical when dealing with the diverse challenges that arise in the workplace. Supervisors need to listen attentively, give employees time to express their views, and respond thoughtfully.

Positivity: Maintaining a positive attitude, even in challenging situations, helps to motivate and inspire team members. Supervisors should lead by example, demonstrating resilience and optimism.

Professionalism: Professional behavior sets the tone for the team. Supervisors should model appropriate conduct, punctuality, and reliability, showing commitment to their role and responsibilities.

Supervisors: Mode of Delivery

The way supervisors deliver their messages significantly impacts how they are received and acted upon by their team members. Effective communication is key to successful leadership at the supervisory level.

Clarity: Supervisors should communicate clearly and concisely, ensuring that their messages are easily understood. This includes giving precise instructions, setting clear expectations, and avoiding jargon or overly complex language.

Consistency: Consistent communication helps to build trust and reliability. Supervisors should ensure that their messages align with the company's policies and values and avoid sending mixed signals.

Supportiveness: When delivering feedback or instructions, supervisors should adopt a supportive tone. Constructive feedback should be framed positively, focusing on ways to improve and offering assistance rather than just highlighting faults.

Active Listening: Supervisors should practice active listening, showing that they value their team members' opinions and concerns. This involves maintaining eye contact, nodding, and providing verbal acknowledgments during conversations.

Adaptability: Different situations and team members may require different communication styles. **Supervisors** should be adaptable, adjusting their tone and approach to suit the context and the individual needs of their team members.

Timeliness: Supervisors should provide feedback and information promptly. Delayed communication can lead to misunderstandings and missed opportunities for improvement.

Encouragement: Regularly recognizing and appreciating employees' efforts and achievements is required. **Supervisors** should provide positive reinforcement to motivate their team and reinforce desired behaviors.

Non-Verbal Communication: Body language, facial expressions, and gestures play a significant role in communication. Supervisors should be aware of their non-verbal cues and ensure they convey confidence, openness, and attentiveness.

Examples of Effective Delivery for Supervisors

Daily Briefings: Starting the day with a brief team meeting to outline daily goals and address any immediate concerns can set a focused and positive tone for the day.

One-on-One Meetings: Regular individual meetings with team members provide opportunities for personalized feedback, goal setting, and professional development discussions.

Open-Door Policy: Encouraging an open-door policy invites employees to voice their concerns, ask questions, and seek guidance, fostering a culture of openness and accessibility.

Written Communication: Sending clear and detailed emails or memos and letters for important updates or instructions ensures that employees have a written reference, reducing the risk of miscommunication. Remember, Proofread the message carefully before sending it to ensure clarity and professionalism, paying extra attention of the letter was formal or systematic.

Feedback Sessions: Holding regular feedback sessions where supervisors highlight both strengths and areas for improvement helps employees grow and feel valued. Furthermore, targeted feedback sessions allow **supervisors** to identify specific areas where an employee can improve. This targeted feedback helps employees focus their development efforts and set achievable goals for growth.

In summary, supervisors should exhibit respectful, empathetic, fair, patient, positive, and professional manners. Their mode of delivery should be clear, consistent, supportive, actively listening, adaptable, timely, encouraging, and mindful of non-verbal communication. By mastering these aspects, supervisors can effectively lead their teams, foster a positive work environment, and drive overall productivity and satisfaction.

Superintendents

Superintendents, who oversee multiple teams or departments, need to exhibit strategic thinking and strong organizational skills. Their behavior should reflect a balance of authority and collaboration, ensuring that they are seen as leaders who can make decisive actions while valuing team input. Superintendents should dress in a manner that commands respect across different levels of the organization, often combining business casual with context-appropriate attire for site visits or meetings with senior management. Their communication style should be articulate and inclusive, capable of addressing diverse audiences and bridging gaps between departments. Superintendents represent the company's commitment to excellence and interdepartmental synergy and innovation.

Superintendents: Manners

Superintendents oversee multiple teams or departments, and their behavior sets the tone for broader organizational culture and operational efficiency. Their manners significantly impact how effectively they can manage and motivate their teams.

Approachability: Superintendents should be accessible and approachable, encouraging open communication and making team members feel comfortable sharing ideas and concerns.

Strategic Thinking: They must exhibit strategic thinking, demonstrating a clear understanding of the company's goals and how departmental efforts align with these objectives.

Collaboration: Fostering a collaborative environment is essential. Superintendents should promote teamwork and cooperation across different departments and units.

Accountability: **Superintendents** must hold themselves and their teams accountable for their actions and outcomes, ensuring that everyone meets their responsibilities and commitments.

Transparency: Being transparent in their decision-making processes builds trust and credibility. **Superintendents** should openly share relevant information and rationales behind key decisions.

Diplomacy: Diplomatic skill for resolving conflicts and navigating the complexities of interdepartmental relations should be key. Superintendents should handle disputes with tact and fairness.

Visionary Leadership: They should inspire their teams with a clear vision and a sense of purpose, motivating employees to work towards long-term goals.

Superintendents: Mode of Delivery

Effective communication at the superintendent level involves conveying complex information clearly and ensuring that strategic messages are understood and acted upon across various departments.

Strategic Clarity: Superintendents should articulate the company's strategic goals and how departmental objectives contribute to these goals, ensuring that everyone understands their role in the bigger picture.

Engagement: Actively engaging with team members through regular meetings and open forums allows **superintendents** to gather feedback, address concerns, and foster a sense of inclusion.

Regular Updates: Providing consistent updates on progress, challenges, and changes keeps everyone informed and aligned. This includes sharing updates on key projects, performance metrics, and strategic initiatives.

Active Listening: Superintendents should practice active listening, showing genuine interest in the input and feedback from team members. This helps build a culture of mutual respect and collaboration.

Empowerment: Empowering team members by delegating authority and responsibility encourages ownership and accountability. Superintendents should provide the necessary support and resources for teams to succeed.

Conflict Resolution: Handling conflicts effectively and promptly ensures that minor issues do not escalate into major problems. Superintendents should mediate disputes and find fair solutions that align with the company's values and goals.

Inspirational Communication: Superintendents should inspire and motivate their teams through their communication, using stories, examples, and a positive tone to highlight successes and future opportunities.

Superintendents Examples of Effective Delivery

Cross-Departmental Workshops: Organizing workshops that bring together different departments to collaborate on common goals fosters a collaborative culture and breaks down silos.

Strategic Planning Sessions: Leading strategic planning sessions with department heads to align on long-term objectives and develop cohesive action plans ensures that everyone is working towards the same goals.

Feedback Loops: Establishing formal feedback loops, such as surveys or suggestion boxes, allows team members to provide input on processes and improvements, making them feel valued and heard.

Mentorship Programs: Implementing mentorship programs where superintendents mentor mid-level managers or promising employees helps in talent development and succession planning.

Performance Reviews: Conducting regular performance reviews that focus on both achievements and areas for improvement provides clarity and direction for team members.

Emergency Preparedness Drills: Leading drills and simulations for emergency situations ensures that all departments are prepared and know how to respond effectively.

In summary, **superintendents** should display approachability, strategic thinking, collaboration, accountability, transparency, diplomacy, and visionary leadership. Their mode of delivery should emphasize strategic clarity, engagement, regular updates, active listening, empowerment, conflict resolution, and inspirational communication. By mastering these aspects, superintendents can effectively lead their departments, drive operational efficiency, and contribute to the overall success of the organization.

Managers

Managers at the highest leadership level must display visionary leadership and strategic foresight. Their behavior should be characterized by decisiveness, ethical conduct, and an inspirational demeanor, driving the company's long-term goals. Managers should dress in professional business attire that reflects their leadership status and sets a standard for the organization. Their communication must be impactful and persuasive, clearly articulating the company's vision, mission, and strategic initiatives. Managers represent the company on a broader scale, often engaging with external stakeholders, partners, and clients. They must embody the company's core values and strategic objectives, fostering a culture of excellence, innovation, and corporate responsibility.

Managers: Manners

Managers occupy high-level leadership positions and are responsible for steering the organization toward its long-term goals. Their manners significantly influence the company culture and overall success.

Visionary Leadership: Managers should embody visionary leadership, setting a clear direction for the organization and inspiring others to follow.

Integrity: Demonstrating unwavering integrity in all actions and decisions fosters trust and sets a strong ethical foundation for the entire organization.

Empowerment: Empowering subordinates by trusting their abilities and giving them autonomy encourages innovation and accountability.

Resilience: Managers should exhibit resilience; a resilient manager focuses on finding solutions rather than dwelling on problems should remain composed and positive in the face of challenges and setbacks, thereby instilling confidence in their teams.

Decisiveness: Managers should always be making prompt and informed decisions for maintaining momentum and driving the organization forward.

Strategic Thinking: Managers must consistently think strategically, considering long-term implications while addressing immediate needs.

Humility: Despite their high position, **managers** should remain humble, acknowledging their team's contributions and being open to feedback and new ideas.

Managers: Mode of Delivery

Effective communication at the managerial level involves influencing, inspiring, and guiding the organization towards its strategic objectives.

Strategic Communication: Managers should communicate the company's vision, mission, and strategic goals clearly, ensuring alignment across all levels of the organization.

Inspirational Messaging: Using inspirational messaging to motivate employees helps foster a strong sense of purpose and commitment to the company's objectives.

Transparent Communication: Managers should maintain transparency in their communication, openly sharing the rationale behind key decisions and organizational changes.

Effective Delegation: Clearly delegating tasks and responsibilities ensures that managers focus on strategic planning while empowering subordinates to execute operational tasks.

Active Listening: Practicing active listening to understand the perspectives and concerns of employees at all levels helps managers make informed decisions and build trust.

Regular Updates: Providing regular updates on the company's performance, market trends, and strategic initiatives keeps employees informed and engaged.

Conflict Resolution: **Managers** should handle conflicts diplomatically, using their authority to mediate disputes and foster a harmonious work environment.

Managers Examples of Effective Delivery

Company-Wide Addresses: Holding quarterly company-wide addresses to update employees on strategic goals, celebrate achievements, and discuss future directions fosters a sense of unity and shared purpose.

Leadership Retreats: Organizing leadership retreats for senior management to align on strategic initiatives and develop cohesive action plans ensures that everyone is working towards the same long-term goals.

Strategic Reviews: Leading regular strategic reviews to assess the progress of long-term initiatives and make necessary adjustments keeps the organization agile and responsive to changes.

Feedback Systems: Implementing robust feedback systems, such as annual surveys and suggestion boxes, allows employees to voice their opinions and contribute to the company's strategic direction.

Recognition Programs: Establishing recognition programs that reward employees for their contributions to strategic initiatives reinforces desired behaviors and motivates continued excellence.

Crisis Communication Plans: Developing and executing effective crisis communication plans ensures that the organization remains resilient and responsive during challenging times.

Mentorship Programs: Creating mentorship programs where managers mentor upcoming leaders within the organization ensures the development of future talent and leadership continuity.

In summary, managers should exhibit visionary leadership, integrity, empowerment, resilience, decisiveness, strategic thinking, and humility. Their mode of delivery should focus on strategic communication, inspirational messaging, transparency, effective delegation, active listening, regular updates, and conflict resolution. By mastering these aspects, managers can effectively lead their organizations, drive strategic success, and foster a culture of excellence and innovation.

At the end, leaders at all levels must behave with integrity and competence, dress appropriately for their role, and communicate effectively. Supervisors should focus on being approachable and practical, superintendents on being strategic and collaborative, and managers on being visionary and inspirational. Each level of leadership should embody and represent the company's values and objectives, ensuring a cohesive and motivated organization.

NAVIGATING CHANGE AND IMPROVEMENT

Navigating Change and Staying Updated

Navigating change effectively requires leaders to maintain flexibility and a proactive mindset. Leaders should start by embracing a growth mindset, recognizing that change is an opportunity for improvement rather than a disruption. To do this, it's crucial to stay informed about industry trends, emerging technologies, and market shifts. Regularly attending industry conferences, webinars, and networking events can provide valuable insights and keep leaders updated on the latest developments. Additionally, subscribing to relevant publications, following thought leaders on social media, and participating in professional groups can help leaders stay ahead of the curve.

Effective communication is vital in navigating change. Leaders should communicate the reasons for change clearly and consistently, ensuring that all team members understand the vision and the benefits of the transition. It's important to involve team members in the change process, soliciting their feedback and addressing their concerns. This inclusive approach not only eases the transition but also fosters a sense of ownership and commitment among employees. Regular updates and transparent communication help in managing expectations and reducing resistance to change.

Adapting to change also involves continuous learning and skill development. Leaders should encourage a culture of learning within their teams, providing opportunities for professional development and training. Leveraging online courses, workshops, and in-house training programs can help team members acquire new skills and stay relevant in their roles. Leaders should also set an example by pursuing their own learning and development, demonstrating the importance of staying updated. Furthermore, fostering resilience and agility within the team is important. Leaders should empower employees to take initiative and make decisions, promoting a culture of innovation and adaptability.

This can be achieved by setting clear goals, providing the necessary resources, and recognizing and rewarding efforts that contribute to successful change management. In summary, navigating change and staying updated require leaders to embrace a growth mindset, maintain effective communication, promote continuous learning, and foster a culture of resilience and agility. By staying informed through various channels and involving their teams in the process, leaders can effectively manage change and ensure their organization remains competitive in a rapidly evolving business environment.

Continuous Improvement

Leaders in both new and established positions can continue driving improvements by fostering a culture of continuous learning and adaptability. In new roles, leaders should start by thoroughly understanding the existing processes, strengths, and weaknesses of their teams. They can achieve this by engaging with team members, seeking their input, and valuing their insights. By promoting open communication and actively listening, leaders can identify areas that need enhancement and develop strategies to address them. Implementing incremental changes and setting clear, achievable goals can help in making steady progress. Additionally, leaders should invest in professional development opportunities for their team, encouraging skill enhancement and staying updated with industry trends and best practices. For leaders in established positions, maintaining momentum for improvements involves regularly revisiting and reassessing existing strategies and processes. These leaders should encourage innovation by creating an environment where team members feel comfortable sharing new ideas and experimenting with novel approaches. Continuous improvement can also be supported by using data and metrics to track progress, identify areas for refinement, and celebrate successes. By remaining flexible and open to change, established leaders can adapt to new challenges and opportunities, ensuring sustained growth and development. Engaging in regular feedback loops and fostering a collaborative spirit can further strengthen the team's commitment to ongoing improvement.

www.ingramcontent.com/pod-product-compliance
Lightning Source LLC
Chambersburg PA
CBHW031924240526
45464CB00022B/674